OFF THE HOOK MARKETING

How to make social media sell for you

Jeffrey G. Molander

Published by
Molander & Associates Inc.
1219 Hull Terrace Suite 2C
Evanston IL 60202

www.molanderassoc.com

Contact the author at: jeff@jeffmolander.com

ISBN: 978-0-9835964-0-0 (hardcover, First Edition)
978-0-9835964-1-7 (softcover)
978-0-9835964-2-4 (ebook)

Library of Congress Catalog Number: 2011913139

Printed in the United States of America

To Diana

Contents

FOREWORD

FEW will question the impact social media is having on people's lives. From breaking news, political revolutions, connecting to old friends, and helping individuals find lost people in emergency situations, social media is touching our lives in meaningful ways every day. But with all the stories you're hearing about Facebook, Twitter, LinkedIn, Google+, and other social networks, the one question you should be asking is, "How can my business make money with social media?"

Does the world need another book describing the opportunity presented by social media? Probably not. Do businesses like yours need a practical way to make social media produce more sales and deepen loyalty? Absolutely.

If you are looking for some black box or secret sauce, don't expect to find it. Social media is giving your customers more choice and information and increasing their expectations. What that means is you need to work harder than ever before. You need to plan great experiences. They don't come by accident. You need to have a solid plan and deliver it with precision.

If you want to make social media sell, you'll need an ally: someone who is uncovering a clear, mature business purpose for social media and who can help you take action on it. Fortunately, you have in your hand just such an ally. In a world filled with so much hype, spin, and charlatanism, Jeff offers brave yet practical answers. For instance, Jeff wisely recommends *designing* experiences to solve customers' problems with social media. Doing so helps customers guide themselves toward products and services they need. Of course, if you're satisfied with hoping lots of Twitter followers or Facebook "likes" earn sales, that's your right. But if you want to sell products or services with social media, read *Off the Hook Marketing*, and do it soon. You'll be glad you did.

Jeff's practical attitude about making social media sell for you is as refreshing as it is useful. He admits, "The idea of conversation is not new. Talking with customers in ways that solves problems is a time-tested, effective way to guide them toward purchase." As it turns out, social media is not a revolution in how business is done. Rather, it is an exciting opportunity to improve on what most of us are already doing—being useful to customers. When Jeff strips away the hype, Facebook starts looking more like a chance to become more relevant to customers' changing needs and less like something you update with posts about your blog or coupons. Seeing the opportunity differently changes everything. It makes taking action easier.

Having known him over the years, I can attest to Jeff's remarkable integrity. His passion for helping others guides his every step. It is with this passion that I hope you can connect to Jeff and find the way to make social media sell for your business.

Bryan Eisenberg
New York Times *best-selling author, international speaker, and Chairman Emeritus, Web Analytics Association*

INTRODUCTION

THERE is a simple way to make social media sell for you, and it is based on a business's approach to marketing itself. That means it's easy to understand. It is also easy to apply. In fact, it's so practical that any business can immediately gain benefits, regardless of the target market, products, services, or size. It is the key to selling more with tools like Facebook, Twitter, podcasts, YouTube, LinkedIn, and blogs.

This book will give you that key. It will empower you to make social media marketing produce sales—starting tomorrow. You may be a one-man or -woman operation, a marketing executive, a student, a business owner, or marketing professional. In the pages ahead, you'll discover a step-by-step way to improve strategies and bypass pitfalls, a way to make social media sell off the hook!

Business owners, you'll learn how to hook new customers more often and serve them in ways that create more referrals and repeat business. Marketing executives, the next time you're pitched on social marketing by a staff member or agency, you'll rest assured that it *will* create leads and sales. Junior or student marketers, this book will help you take "social media, the opportunity" and turn it into a new job or pay raise.

Is there more to social media than grabbing at customers' attention, answering their complaints in a new way, or handing out coupons and discounts wherever and whenever they flock online? Could social media marketing be a chance to help customers get what they need into their hands—your products and services? The truth is this: most people dipping their toes into social media waters aren't getting the results they want. Web measurement luminary Avinash Kaushik once noticed how, for most people, social media is like teen sex. Everyone wants to do it, but no one actually knows how, and when it's finally done—surprise—it's not what they expected! But social media can be a more powerful servant to your business. It *will* be. For instance, you don't have to cut prices and struggle to maintain profit. Social media can help you escape the pricing trap. I'll show you how. But you'll need to take action on the plain truth.

Design to Sell

When I sat down to write this book, I noticed something shocking right away. Many businesses told me that sales are "just happening." They write blog stories, upload videos, Tweet, post on Facebook, and so on, and sales happen. The folks I was interviewing were uploading videos of something outrageous, or poking fun at themselves on YouTube. Things went viral and caused sales to increase. Now, they couldn't *prove* that social media was working. It just *had* to be. Even when they were already creating demand for products—using TV or radio spots, direct mail or other Web marketing—social media was always a winner. It never failed to deliver. Why? Because it was social media, silly! But then I began interviewing people who actually were creating leads and sales with social media. *They could prove it,* and they all told me the same thing.

I wasn't crazy. I was right to be suspicious. Sales don't "just happen." They told me their secret to success is *designing* social media to cause sales. They started explaining to me how trusting *traditional* business instincts more often is helping them *sell* more often. To my surprise, these businesses are spending *less* time seeking customers' attention with social media and more time helping customers *solve problems*, hooking them with answers, and keeping them on the line until they purchase.

The more I learned about how these businesses succeed, the more I started thinking about fishing. Heh, not because I wanted a day off, but because of what happens when people go fishing.

Think about the last time you went fishing—with actually catching fish in mind! Whether alone or with someone, you probably gave thought to how you would *attract* fish—what bait you will use. But attracting the fish is only the beginning, isn't it? Once you find a school of fish, attracting one is easy. You use bait like corn, worms, buzzbaits, spinners, jigs, minnows, squid, or shrimp— whatever. But then the *real* work begins. Eventually you get a bite and have a chance to set the hook. If you're lucky, you hooked one good. If you're not, you're like me, I'm afraid! But once a fish is hooked, you have more work to do. You need to keep 'em on the line and land 'em, and that's precisely how it works in social media.

Shift Focus

Getting customers to bite on Facebook, Twitter, or a blog is the easy part. Earning a *sale* from them is the hard part. Yes, or yes? So that makes it smart to invest *more* of your precious time in mastering that part. This means shifting focus.

For instance, what separates professional tournament fishermen from the novices? Believe it or not, it's not the fancy equipment. My buddy David (a semi-pro bass fisherman) let me in on the secret. Catching *more* big fish more often means spending *less* time worrying about attracting them. In other words, you better learn how set the hook in the fish's mouth before anything else. It's critical to spend time learning and practicing, not to mention keeping the fish on the line ("tip up, tip up!") and getting 'em into the boat. ("Crikey, where's that net?!") Otherwise you risk being surrounded by fish, only to keep missing the bite. You risk trying to set the hook over and over and to keep missing over and over; landing fewer fish. You'll get "blanked" or "skunked," as my dad would say. Now, think about how *you* are using social media. Sound familiar?

Remember the first time you tried to set the hook on a fish? You missed, didn't ya'? And it took a while to get it right. But once you did, you caught one, and it felt *great*. Well, it's the same with social media marketing. Attracting customers is relatively easy. Therefore, it should be taking up *less* of your time. Getting customers to bite on Facebook, Twitter, or a blog and earning a *sale* from them is the hard part. That means this part should occupy *more* of your precious time.

But rock star gurus claim sales "just happen." All that's needed is blogging "compelling content" or being "more transparent" or updating Facebook "x" times per day, but successful social sellers know better. Customers' attention is fleeting. You'd better know how to set a hook and have the skills needed to get that customer into the boat, and that's *never* been easy. Sure, sometimes it takes just a few seconds to reel customers in. Other times it takes a few months. Like your uncle always told you, "That's why they call it fishing, not catching!" Success requires technique.

That's why I've written this book. I'll teach you that technique and help you refocus your time investment. Everyone I interviewed in this book told me the same, essential story: The trick to making social media sell is, yes, finding and attracting customers. But the real key is to spend time perfecting *ways to land them*, and that's done by helping customers solve everyday problems; that's what this book is about.

How to Read This Book

I've organized the book in a way that's easy to read and put to quick use. When I explain a concept or principle, I bring it to life by offering examples of successful companies. I'll also introduce you to the people who run them, like Amanda Kinsella of Logan Services, a Dayton, Ohio–based residential air conditioning and heating business. She's using Facebook to generate a constant flow of local leads. You'll also meet savvy marketers like Rachel Farris of PetRelocation .com, who uses blogging to quickly generate leads. She's delivering more prospects—that convert more often—to her lean-and-mean sales team. You'll also meet Ryan Safady. When he's not renting Lamborghini cars and Boeing business jets on his blog, he's selling fabric to do-it-yourself crafters using Facebook. By day, he rents luxury cars, yachts, homes, and planes at his start-up company, Imagine Lifestyles. By night he's selling novelty fabrics at his family's fifty-year-old New Jersey–based fabric store. He's using social media to sell off the hook, too.

Of course, you'll meet large, multi-channel, product-focused public companies like rural lifestyle and gardening retailer Tractor Supply Company. In partnership with *The Chicken Whisperer*, TSC's Andrew Heltsley is finding ways to use video and blogging to attract new customers, increase referrals, and sell more products online and in-store. You'll learn the latest successes of small business powerhouse Intuit as their team finds new ways to sell using Facebook. I'll also tell a handful of horror stories exposing what doesn't work. We'll learn what could have been done differently to improve the outcome.

Each chapter shows you how leading businesses are investing time, energy, and money into social media marketing in ways that create more leads and sales. But I'm also aiming at provoking action in your everyday life. That's why most of the chapters conclude with action-oriented reflection questions.

Chapter 1 gives you glimpses into the lives of businesses that are selling off the hook. You'll meet remarkable product and service marketers who are quietly thriving. Chapter 2 focuses on the good stuff: how to start capturing more sales using social media marketing. We'll learn how selling someone something doesn't require engagement, conversation, and a relationship, rather, how engagement, conversation, and relationships are created by selling them something! *And* you'll learn two practical, easy-to-remember success principles that always get results.

Chapter 3 will help you move beyond listening to customers and start ***translating*** their evolving needs. For instance, you'll learn how prompting customers to signal what they're most interested in, when, where, and why leads to more sales, especially when mixed with publishing useful, relevant tools and information that fit customers' buying contexts. I'll even show you how to start designing processes that guide customers toward destinations they choose—your products and services.

Chapter 4 explains why most businesses struggle to make social media marketing sell. This is where we focus on overcoming roadblocks to success. You'll have some fun in this chapter. You might even feel a bit satisfied as we take aim at popular social media best practices that often do more harm than good.

Chapter 5 will help you steer clear of pitfalls being thrown at you by a variety of forces. For instance, we'll learn how "influencing the influencers" may not be the Holy Grail that gurus say it is and how molding customers' behavior is a more practical way to induce sales.

Chapter 6 is where we get action-oriented. I'll show you how to put everything to work, starting now. I'll give tips on maximizing your own personal time investments and larger strategies. You'll learn practical, "no-bull" methods to make social media produce sales without the headaches. You'll learn how easy it is to make each social tactic connect to the sales funnel. The concluding chapter cements your new perspective and sends you off with the needed motivation. You'll have the tools and confidence needed to solve customers' problems like never before.

And by the way, all of my ideas are weighted the same no matter how you choose to use them—in part or in whole. You bring your own strengths and weaknesses to this book, so I encourage you to make creative use of my tips. Also, when I use the terms *business, company,* and *organization* in this book, I'm really talking about any kind of entity or individual. Just the same, when I use the terms *buyer* and *customer,* I also means subscribers, voters, patients, donors, applicants, or worshipers. The principles you'll learn are flexible enough to be applied widely.

Just think about it for a moment: won't it feel great to *sell* using social media, to know that everything you're doing will ultimately result in leads and sales? Whether you're a one-person operation or a multi-billion dollar corporation, today's successful social media marketer pulls a paycheck by *generating sales.* They get paid to sell off the hook, period. Now let's get going!

CHAPTER 1

GENERATE LEADS AND MAKE SALES NOW

"You don't sell someone something by engagement,
conversation, and relationship.
You create engagement, conversation,
and relationships by selling them something."

Bob Hoffman
"The Ad Contrarian"
CEO, Hoffman Lewis

Selling Bracelets with Blogs

MEET Jenna White, of Lauren's Hope (www.laurenshope.com), a manufacturer and retailer of designer medical identification "alert" bracelets. She's a one-woman marketing juggernaut who's increasing year-over-year sales by 40 percent using Facebook and a blog. How? By helping new customers find solutions to problems. In return, she's earning the business of skeptical, reluctant customer groups. She's finding new ways to solve an old problem—eliminating barriers between potential customers and her products. She's selling off the hook.

For millions of people, it's vital to wear a medical identification bracelet.

From diabetes to Alzheimer's to having a food allergy, an increasing number of Americans need protection from an increasing number of threats. In emergencies, bracelets save lives or help avoid unnecessary (or even damaging) medical procedures. First responders and emergency room doctors need to know *exactly* what they're dealing with, immediately.

That should be enough reason to wear some kind of ID. But too often it's not. Neither is this seemingly must-have item very popular. Demand is actually weak, mostly because traditional medical alert bracelets draw attention to illness and lack fashion sense; they're just plain unappealing. Enter Lauren's Hope, a small business providing stylish, attractive, and functional medical ID jewelry to men, women, and children. This 15-employee business sells bracelets, necklaces, and specialty items like temporary medical ID tattoos, dog tag necklaces, and ankle bracelets.

Historically, the company markets itself at trade shows, using direct mail (purchasing lists), appearing at craft shows, participating in health-related support groups, and using a public relations agency. In 2000, the company launched into e-commerce, but until White's arrival, Lauren's Hope wasn't fully positioned as a strong online seller. Namely, the company wasn't being discovered by new customers via the Web often enough. Even with increasing numbers of potential customers seeking knowledge about ID products online, this seller wasn't popping onto buyers' radars often enough.

After insisting to company founders that she saw potential to make serious improvements, White began blogging in 2010, but she didn't focus her attention on learning how to operate blog software or install plugins. Sure, she knew the technical details were all necessary, but they wouldn't help her generate sales. This one-woman marketing department realized something important.

Knowing how to "do social media" is worthless without knowing how to *design it* to produce sales. Having a plan matters.

"While my partner and I believe we're good at what we do, we're also smart enough to realize what we're not good at," says co-founder LeAnn Carlson. "Jenna brought our weak search engine position to light, but more importantly, she brought us solutions!"

Today, Lauren's Hope is netting more sales because White uses her blog to nurture *behavior*. While competitors are occupying prospects' time by "engaging" them, she's publishing useful information that *solves their problems*, and she's mixing in traditional marketing concepts like promotions. *That* is how her company is generating sales with tools like Facebook and blogs. Now doesn't that sound like something *your* business can do? Of course it does.

Today, White's e-commerce and informational Web sites are being discovered by more prospects, more often, and her blogging is generating an increasing number of sales because she's priming her pump. Lauren's Hope is earning meaningful relationships with prospects—*even when they're not ready to buy*. And when the prospect *is* ready to purchase a medical ID, White isn't just top-of-mind. She's become woven into the fabric of her prospects' lives; she's always ready with a call to action.

For instance, White cooked up a practical promotional idea called Free Stuff Friday. She offers three lucky, randomly selected winners the chance to have their pick of fancy ID bracelets or necklaces—it's a simple giveaway promotion. But in return, she earns a subscriber to her blog (an e-mail address), a fan of her Facebook page, and a story about Lauren's Hope posted on the contest participants' blog. In essence, this earns White a sales lead in return for giving her prospect a chance at a free product. She acquires a relationship with a potential customer who's actively demonstrating need for her product. And by tapping into her participants' Facebook networks with compelling calls to action, she's earning access to more potential customers. This is driving increasing numbers of prospective customers to sign up for Free Stuff Friday and download handy "wallet card" medical alert guides among other behaviors. In other words, prospects are recruiting more prospects!

"Once someone has become a blog subscriber, they are now exposed to promotions, useful tips, information on what to engrave on IDs, customer stories, guest blog posts from customers, charities, and other educational Web sites," says White, who is finding new ways to convert her leads over time. "As evidenced by the comments prospects and customers are leaving on blog posts, being exposed to the conditions and needs of fellow medical ID wearers has formed quite a strong community."

Using these kinds of clever-but-traditional marketing ideas, White earned fifteen hundred subscribers within the first five months of blogging. Today, her prospecting database is nearly two thousand prospects strong, and it's growing every week.

Make no mistake: White is building a prospecting list, and she's doing it using some of the oldest tricks in the book—a giveaway promotion, for instance, an "ethical bribe," if you will. These goodhearted gestures are the company's hook. This smart strategy gives Lauren's Hope a reason to reconnect with people that do not win the contest. At the same time, it gives contest participants incentive to help build the company's prospecting list. These promotions serve everyone's interest.

Promotions are but one of White's secret weapons. She's also a problem solver for a wide range of potential customers. For instance, one segment of White's potential customers already uses medical IDs. But they're not aware of the elegant, beautiful options Lauren's Hope presents. Other times these prospects are wearing IDs that do not contain proper medical information, and it's White's job to point that out by offering a specific solution—what information needs to be engraved, when, and how. Blogging offers that opportunity. Rather than advertising what she has for sale, she's answering important, related questions. She's solving problems that potential customers are actively seeking answers to.

"We are not only providing customers with useful information," says White. "Social media gives us a new chance to answer their questions on an emotional level."

Another customer segment for Lauren's Hope has yet to realize it should be wearing a medical ID. These prospects often turn to the Web for information on coping with, treating, and overcoming various health conditions and diseases. White is attracting these prospects with stories and tips focusing on risks associated with not wearing an ID in specific situations. Everyday events like "Your child has a bee sting allergy and, while at a friend's house, is stung by a bee" or "You are at risk for a stroke and are in a setting where people are unfamiliar with the symptoms." White wisely recommends wearing an ID if "you are a caregiver of an older adult and are in an accident … unable to communicate your responsibilities."

All of these real-life scenarios give White fertile ground to plant seeds— talk about solutions, educate, and provide answers to people who need them.

Sometimes she provides prospects with a better way to protect themselves in case of emergency. Other times she's giving advice on more elegant, fun, or sharp ways for people to stay safe.

When customers understand their problems more clearly, they're better equipped to find the right solutions, and that includes relevant products and services.

Yes, White blogs about new products on occasion, but she focuses on meaningful stories and useful information. She's always finding new ways to connect her blog to a process that captures and nurtures demand: a system **designed** to sell off the hook.

> *When customers understand their problems more clearly, they're better equipped to find the right solutions, and that includes relevant products and services.*

In essence, Lauren's Hope is marketing a product that an increasing number of people need. But those people often don't want or like IDs—even if one can save their life. The very idea of medical ID jewelry conjures up unappealing emotions, and that's why White started viewing social media as an opportunity: a chance to do what the company does best—that is, help people solve a variety of problems in a compassionate, empathetic, and heartwarming way.

Best of all, White is experiencing how social media can empower her. She sees how it can scale her precious time across thousands of prospects, and she's jumping at the opportunity. Today, social media is helping her prove what seemed unprovable to customers: that it *is* possible to look good, stay safe, and avoid medical catastrophes all at the same time. White is not only getting the word out about products and benefits: she's slowly but surely earning the business of skeptical, reluctant customers. She's finding new ways to solve an old problem— eliminating barriers between customers and Lauren's Hope's products.

Selling Swimming Pools
with Social Media

Marcus Sheridan is selling more fiberglass swimming pools than any other local pool retailer in North America. His blog is so popular, influential, and controversial that every major equipment manufacturer is courting him for some kind of strategic alliance. He's even selling installation and equipment leads to pool and spa companies across America, creating new revenue streams. And to top it off, his company no longer depends on leads from manufacturers. What's his secret? Sheridan says it's all thanks to social media—that is, a focus on making social sell and a bit of elbow grease.

In 2006, the top national fiberglass pool company sold five hundred pools. In 2009, it sold thirty-five. Lack of consumer spending is either killing off or driving half of America's pool installers into the red. Pools and spas are luxury items; they're what people want, not what they need. But Sheridan's River Pools and Spas is thriving. In 2007, the business spent over $250,000 in advertising to net roughly $4.5 million in sales. In 2010, it spent $40,000 to achieve the same sales number, not to mention winning 15 percent more bids and dramatically shortening the sales cycle, all during the greatest economic slowdown since the Great Depression. Sheridan and his cofounders, Jim Spiess and Jason Hughes, are living the dream.

"It's all because of content," says Sheridan, who is generating local leads, increasing profit margin, and closing sales faster using his blog.

"I'd been going on sales appointments and teaching people about pools for years," reflects Sheridan, who started-up the Virginia-based company in 2001. "I'd sit down at the kitchen table with my customer and spend a couple hours teaching them about pools. Eventually I'd get around to spending thirty minutes trying to *sell* them a pool. That never made sense to me. I knew it was the wrong methodology."

"With blogging, I quickly realized how I could do all the teaching *before* I ever even met the prospect. They could meet me, get to know me by name ... get to know my thoughts, my feelings, and my approach to swimming pools," says Sheridan, who suddenly realized it *was* possible to make every minute of his day more productive by *publishing his lessons* on the Web.

Sheridan's big "ah-ha" was that blogging *could* serve a real purpose for his business. On that fateful day he started making blogging a useful part of his daily life, he saw a way—a simple process—to make Web publishing serve River Pools and Spas: to help grow it. He never looked back.

How to Start Generating Local Leads with a Blog

"In 2009, I said, 'Okay, I need to figure out a way to get more leads.' I had 15–20 percent of the leads that I had previously," says Sheridan, who needs to sell a minimum of 80 pools a year to break even. "If I can't meet that number, I'm sunk."

Sheridan quickly realized he wasn't going to get the leads he needed to survive from his manufacturers. In fact, he felt far too dependent on manufacturers, and that was a problem, as was the idea of merely breaking even. He and his two partners have families to feed. So he began to blog based on questions he was getting from customers.

"Our approach was simple: we wrote down every question that's ever been asked to us by customers. We didn't care how generic or broad the questions were. We wrote all the questions down. These quickly became the titles of our blog posts," Sheridan says in his typical, blunt style.

"We took all the questions and answered them as only we can do: really candidly. That's what prospects want. Within the first year of blogging, I wrote something like two articles a week, which isn't prolific ... but I'm a guy that's busy selling pools and running a business," says Sheridan, who admits he wasn't a very good writer.

> *"Our approach was simple: we wrote down every question that's ever been asked to us by customers. [...] These quickly became the titles of our blog posts."*

"But then I figured out what my voice was … and that I just needed to write like I talk. And I eventually got pretty good at it. And then our Web site just exploded. Of course, I started getting visitors from all over the world. But I was also getting a lot of traffic from within my region—*that I probably would not have gotten* if I was using some other type of medium."

It worked. Sheridan knew that early-stage prospects don't turn to Yellow Pages or TV ads for advice about pools. Neither do they typically turn to manufacturers for advice. When customers begin to consider buying an in-ground, fiberglass pool, they're hungry for answers to a variety of questions, and they turn to one resource time and time again: the Web.

"By publishing all those 'long tail,' niche questions that we've been asked constantly … over the course of ten years … all of a sudden I had a very, very dominant keyword 'footprint' in search engines like Google. I was scoring huge benefits on my e-commerce and blog sites. And when the blog started to grow in popularity, inbound links started to come. People were citing us as a resource. Then referrals started to grow. It was a domino effect," says Sheridan.

Sheridan understands two important facts. First, the Web is flooded with prospects seeking specific *answers*. No, they're not ready to buy yet. They're hunting knowledge, and they're considering a purchase. In early stages, they're simply trying to discover authoritative, trustworthy advice before they buy. The social Web is a goldmine of opportunity. All you need is the focus, tools, and dedication to *nurture* prospects along—and ultimately be there to capture the sale.

Secondly, Sheridan realizes knowledge sharing alone doesn't generate sales. That's why he constantly asks serious prospects for something *in return for* the knowledge he shares. Sometimes it's information on his blog. Other times it's a professionally produced, educational DVD or an e-book. In any case, River Pools and Spas doesn't give away the store. The business asks prospects to share *who* they are and *where they are* in the purchase consideration process. Sheridan qualifies each of his leads.

How to Increase Profit Margins with a Blog

"I'm *always* the highest number. Sure, I lose jobs, and that's okay," says Sheridan as he discusses his market position. "For instance, I've got a local competitor in the Richmond area. He needs to sell 2.5 pools for every one of mine ... to make the same amount of money I do. Which is the better business model?"

Sheridan says he's the highest price in town, but he's *still* selling more pools—even when his competitors are beating him on quotes. Not being the low-ball bidder suits him just fine, and it's all because his blog (www.riverpool sandspas.com/blog) is part of a higher caliber consultative selling process. Said plainly, he "gives more to get more" from customers, and the people he wants to do business with see a *clear* difference between River Pools and Spas and the rest of the pack.

"My local customers realize very quickly that I'm the voice of the fiberglass pool industry," says a modest but confident Sheridan. "They have an opportunity to buy from a brutally honest authority or some guy that's never given them one valuable bit of information in their life—except a low price tag. Well, many times they're going to choose our company."

"It's not about being the cheapest guy. I don't talk about lowest prices *ever*. I'm not interested in that at all," says Sheridan, and he doesn't shrink from the challenge of backing up that high sticker price with quality products and services. He knows that's an age-old business challenge. Every business owner and brand has been forced to grapple with quality expectations of customers. River Pool and Spas is stepping up to the plate and swinging for the fences.

Blogging to Shorten Sales Cycles

Sheridan doesn't stop at keeping profit margins high. He works tirelessly to ensure prospects choose River Pools and Spas without shopping around. Blogging literally lowers the number of competitive quotes his prospects need to satisfy thirst for "proper due diligence." Don't believe it? Sheridan says he's living proof.

"The problem is this: In this economy, everyone thinks they can get the deal of a lifetime, especially when they're dealing with a luxury item like a landscaper or a pool guy. These are things you don't have to have. So the homeowner thinks they can beat the living snot out of you because they know you're desperate for the work," says Sheridan, who points out this dynamic is not limited to the pool industry.

"So here's my solution: I want my prospect to be so enamored with me; so in love with my content; so in love with the value I've given them, that *they don't shop*. Literally. And I get it all the time. I met with three people last week. All three prospects bought. You know how many got a second quote? Zero. That doesn't happen in the pool industry. Okay, honestly, one of the leads was going to get one. But she changed her tune when I reminded her who was 'there for her' as her guide before she decided to make the investment. But those three sales? They were home runs," says Sheridan, who seems endlessly enthusiastic.

"I literally tell hot prospects, 'You have read 200 pages of my Web site. You've done more due diligence than 90 percent of the people who buy pools. Why do you feel like you need to do more?' And all the time people say, 'You're right,' because I'm giving them the chance to do their due diligence. In fact, I want them to do their homework *before I get to their house*."

"Look ... when I go on a sales call, I'm not going there to *teach* about pools," says Sheridan. "I'm going there to *sell* a pool to someone I've already gained the trust of—because of the content on my blog."

Sheridan points out how businesses he competes with often run average or below-average lead-nurturing processes. For instance, he sees businesses sending prospects trite, meaningless e-mails saying, "Thanks for contacting our company, we appreciate it, we'll be in touch soon."

Sheridan candidly says, "Well ... I don't believe in that." Instead, this savvy salesman knows all leads have one, two, or even three deal-breaking—or deal-making—concerns, and this spells opportunity.

"Let's say I have a lead, and that lead identifies a specific set of obstacles to buying," says Sheridan. "I help prospects get comfortable with each concern by placing articles I've written into each of my *personalized* follow-up e-mails. In addition to responding to their specific issues, I send out a standard set of information to prospects. They get my fifty-page e-book (which is just a compilation of articles I've written). They get my reference list, five links to three or four videos, two other articles."

"I'm make sure that each prospect is so well informed—by the time I get in their house—that it's *impossible* for them not to know me. To really 'get' me. To know my products, the process, the delivery. *Everything* that makes River Pools and Spas unique, worth doing business with," says Sheridan.

"So when I get to the kitchen table, I'm not teaching any longer. *I'm there to sell*. To me, that's what content marketing is all about. It's the greatest sales tool in the world," says Sheridan with a smile.

Blogging Works for Local Marketers

"I see many local small businesses saying, 'I don't want to blog because I'm just going to get visitors from outside of my area.' Frankly, that's just a bad attitude. And worse, it's not true. I'm living proof. But I'm convinced … people with this attitude aren't seeing content as a useful, purposeful tool," says Sheridan, who believes blogging is "the greatest sales tool in the world—when it's squarely *aligned* with sales processes."

For instance, Sheridan says to consider a search engine term his buyers often use: "Fiberglass versus vinyl liner pools which is better." A prospect typing this phrase into Google is a pretty serious pool buyer, and Sheridan is writing content to match this search query.

Realistically speaking, out of one thousand people who type that into Google, "Maybe five are going to be from Maryland or five will be from Virginia," says Sheridan. "But I'll *take* those five or ten. I'll play those numbers."

"Think of it this way," he says. "It's likely none of River Pool and Spas competitors is going to discover an early-stage lead from a manufacturer or general advertisement. And if a competitor *does* run into the prospect, they'll often send them toward 'informational dead ends.' Even today, swimming pool manufacturers aren't very good at providing the most basic, fundamental answers—let alone the brutally honest kind. In fact they're nearly absent in helping early-stage customers." So Sheridan is jumping right in, head first, with Web sites that are designed to sell, and step 1 is educating customers as part of a lead-nurturing program.

"There are pool companies out there that don't get one thousand visits per year. That's a fact. And yesterday I got a couple of thousand visits alone," says Sheridan. "I wrote two articles that were pretty controversial, I admit. One was addressing a serious problem in the industry that evoked strong thoughts and reactions. I had tons of comments rolling in. Does this kind of thing help me sell pools? You bet it does. And then some."

"When I first got into blogging, I realized search engine optimization has nothing to do with blogging," says an exuberant Sheridan. "It has everything to do with *selling*."

Sheridan is a go-getter by nature, and he's out to dominate his territory. But he's eager to share. That's why he teaches other business owners how to sell with social tools like Facebook, Twitter, and blogs. His business blog has cast him as the nation's leading fiberglass pool expert, bar none, but he also publishes TheSalesLion.com, where he helps small-business owners generate more leads, more often, across multiple industries. Be sure to tune in!

Go Fish!

I'd go fishing with Jenna White and Marcus Sheridan any day because they're laser-focused on hooking customers, keeping them on the line, and landing 'em. They're not afraid to rely on instinct—traditional sales skills and long-standing marketing ideas. Their businesses are becoming known, differentiating, increasing sales, and keeping more customers—all by *diagnosing and solving customer problems*. They aren't just earning customers' attention in places like Facebook: they're doing something with it.

As pro bass fisherman Babe Winkelman was fond of saying, "To catch more fish, think like one." It sounds overly simplistic, but if you've ever had a successful day on the water, you know it's true. Once you understand the simple, instinctual preferences of fish, you'll have less trouble attracting them to your lure, hooking, and landing them.

> *When chasing customers using social media, we tend to focus on technology. But it's actually a big distraction. Focus on solving customers problems instead.*

Just like customers, fish are purpose-driven. They've got problems to fix—namely eating and not being eaten. Now, I know your customers aren't fish, and this will be the last fishing metaphor, I promise, but when people go fishing, most of them focus on things like water temperature, clarity, proper bait, the weather—the environment. They don't tend to focus on what's *really* driving the fish: hunger and fear. When chasing customers in social spaces, people tend to do the same thing. For instance, they focus on the technical aspects of Facebook or Twitter. They look to ideas like number of updates or posts to make per week. But pros like Jenna White and Marcus Sheridan know that the technology is actually a huge distraction, and that's why they focus on *problems* customers face. White and Sheridan realize that helping customers to *get things done* is where to focus.

For instance, most buyers have practical, easy-to-understand problems that need solving. From advice on raising kids to divorce or managing finances, people are constantly seeking answers to problems because we humans don't plan much. Instead, we tend to react to whatever life throws at us, and we're increasingly turning to friends, family, and other credible sources to make purchase decisions. Okay. Got it. So now what?

Well, smart marketers are "chumming the water"—making sure answers and bits of yummy advice (bait) are discoverable in search engines. They're making sure these tips are portable and easily shared by customers with others, and they're baiting customers with answers to problems, sometimes mixing in promotions, free trials and other goodies. Of course, they never forget to set the hook by asking customers to exchange a bit of information about themselves. Keeping customers from wriggling off the hook is where things like content marketing come into play. We'll talk more about all of these concepts in the next chapter. For now, let's focus on how landing more sales, more often is a matter of solving problems for customers, and keep in mind how learning the technical ins and outs is *not* the secret sauce.

PetRelocation.com: Making Social Media Sell

Until recently, Rachel Farris was a one-woman marketing extravaganza, and she's been selling off the hook with social media since the start. She's using tools like blogs, YouTube, and Facebook to generate 200 leads per day for Austin-based business PetRelocation.com. The company's "white glove" pet relocation services cost between $1,200 and $6,000. On an average day, social media is sending her $12,000 to $15,000 in new accounts. She's managed this all while eliminating spending on the company's sole source of advertising—pay-per-click Google ads. Yet Farris and a newly hired counterpart are only getting warmed up.

What's her secret? Social media serves her. Farris doesn't serve it. Her success is based on better ways of working with social media tools like Facebook and Twitter—simple guide rails she's created. Think of it as preplanned marketing that guides customers toward destinations they (customers) choose, and those destinations include PetRelocation.com's products and services.

Maybe you're wondering how often Farris updates PetRelocation.com's Facebook profile or how much blog or video content she is producing, and how often. How many adorable pet photos is she posting, and to where? You may be surprised to learn Farris is not meeting more customers by having answers to these questions. Having hoards of Facebook fans isn't earning her more sales either. She isn't investing time worrying about being "liked" a lot or at a certain ratio or frequency, and she doesn't know how much each of her Facebook fans are worth because these are not the keys to success.

There's no such thing as a silver bullet, but there is a simple system—a practical way to *design* social media to sell off the hook—and that's Farris's secret.

PetRelocation.com is netting more sales because Farris is focusing tools like blogs on creating purposeful *behavior*, not "engagement." She works diligently at *translating* customers' evolving needs, not sending them messages or offering discounts, and she's publishing useful knowledge that **solves customers' problems**.

Farris isn't burdened by social media; she's empowered by it. It serves a mature purpose—to sell. She makes time for social media marketing without fear or anxiety. Farris and her colleague aren't fooling around with social media; they're building a business on it, and so can you.

Selling Confidence

"People always say to me, 'It must be so fun to work at a pet company,'" says Farris, PetRelocation.com's director of operations. "They love their pets ... and so they assume it would be fun to help relocate pets all day long for a living."

"But the fact is our customers are *moving*. They're relocating all over the world with their pets. And honestly, it ranks right up there with weddings and funerals ... in terms of the stress created by planning. Once they look into it a bit, people don't like thinking about actually doing it," says Farris, whose company has specialized in international relocation since 2004.

PetRelocation.com's target market is a tough nut to crack. Once customers realize relocation is only a matter of time, they turn to the Web for answers. They're busy, working professionals who love their pets. Understandably, they need to move with as little stress as possible, but they quickly discover government agencies to be dealt with, cultural differences, and all kinds of confusing signals. "Facts" start coming from family friends and misleading sources on the Web. This sometimes panics pet owners, causing them to be emotionally torn. Should they even try to take their pet?

With customers' stress in mind, this fast-growing, nineteen-employee–strong company is responding boldly. Everything Farris does online gives potential customers *confidence*, but not in how well the business can relocate a pet for them; instead, she is proving something more important—that is, the idea that relocating a pet across continents *can* be done smoothly and successfully, joyfully and with confidence.

"Our hands-down most popular blog post is rather dry," explains Farris, who says the path to making an emotional connection with people often involves putting out fires.

"The post (www.oth.me/petrelo) explains how to get a specific type of health certificate issued by your veterinarian and then stamped by the state USDA office," she says. "People have tons of questions about how to issue this, who can issue it, where to obtain the document, when it is needed, and so on. This gives us a great opportunity to be a source of authority on something that is confusing and stressful for most people."

With the support of PetRelocation.com's founder, Farris is giving away her service team's best-kept secrets. She blogs tips and produces videos on what they do and how they do it for customers. Yes, she's doing it to create awareness of PetRelocation.com across the vast social Web. But it's also part of a larger plan to sell off the hook.

Solve Problems, Make Sales

Today, PetRelocation.com is trouncing the competition by becoming *the* authoritative source on how to successfully relocate pets. The small businesses' e-commerce and informational Web sites are being discovered by prospects more often, and they're generating more leads because the company is providing answers to very specific questions, like how to move specific kinds of pets to specific destinations without headaches. The company is solving problems for pet owners, and in return, it's earning leads.

Sure, PetRelocation.com's blog and video tips are published to the Web in hopes of being noticed. But Farris isn't limiting herself to getting the attention of new customers; she is setting the bar one notch higher. Her approach is *designed* to help the company:

1. Get *discovered* in search engines by people looking for help with pet relocation *and*
2. *Solve problems* for prospective customers that deliver meaning—practical know-how that also taps into emotional benefits, *and*
3. Discover customers' *changing needs* and cater to them in ways that sell.

Get Discovered the Easy Way

Ultimately, PetRelocation.com's approach to what's being called "content marketing" is driven by a process. The company aims to be discovered within search engines like Google. To do that, Farris is constantly demonstrating *how* PetRelocation.com's experts are solving problems. This is a reliable way to attract, bond with, and provide value to prospects. Farris works diligently to make sure her blog is *constantly* being discovered by people who are planning to relocate a pet.

For instance, she knows people are out there seeking answers to pressing questions, so she provides a free "Ask an Expert" Web form that collects a steady stream of inbound questions—all using very relevant, specific words and phrases that "we could never anticipate," says Farris. These phrases are detailed, often niche expressions of customer need. Being able to access *exactly how customers are asking questions* gives her insight on what, when, and why to blog. It increases PetRelocation.com's chances of getting found by potential customers using search engines.

Here is how it works: Each day, questions from the Ask the Expert form are delivered to a PetRelocation.com expert via an e-mail alert. Inside the message is the question being submitted and a Web link to the company's blog management system. Experts simply read the question, click the link, answer the question with appropriate information, and hit submit. This "knowledge tidbit" is automatically converted into a keyword-rich, properly titled blog post using a tool from blogware company Compendium LLC.

One recent question was how to move a dog from Japan to Quito, Ecuador. Things like microchip IDs, vaccinations, health certificates, and quarantines are involved. Another answer-seeker fell in love with a puppy in Thailand and wants to bring her back to Germany. She has obtained microchip identification and vaccinations but needs to know what else Germany requires. Another question dealt with moving a pet rabbit from Kenya to Dubai. Yet another asks about transporting reptiles domestically via U.S. airlines. Yet another inquiry features a woman named Malika who "travels to Dakar, Senegal, for extended periods and would like to know if it is possible to take my lovely Blue Heeler, Zeta, with me and what the procedural steps would be?"

Each of these questions and responses are displaying on PetRelocation.com's blog site, linking to more information on "pet import rules and requirements" by country, for instance. PetRelocation.com constantly makes easy-to-understand answers available, ready to be discovered by people seeking the same answers. Some are quirky, some commonplace, but all of them are being constantly discovered by search engines and the pet owners who use them. That's one way PetRelocation.com receives a steady stream of answer-seeking prospects.

Blogs and Video That Sell

But Farris is hungry. She wants more answer seekers hitting her Web site. So she produces helpful, authoritative blog stories and videos focusing on useful tips for pet owners. They're easy to produce because they're based on her service team's success stories. They're simple and fun to whip up. For instance, Phoebe is a fourteen-year-old Belgian Malinois. This recent, slightly older customer needed to be handled with care. She was moved with great success. It was a perfect excuse for PetRelocation.com to write-up some quick tips on relocating older dogs.

Should one even attempt to move an aging pet? How do you make the call? If yes, what are some quick tips on how to pull it off successfully? Farris is always asking herself, "What other excuses do we have for talking about how-to tips?" That's how the company cooked up its "Pet Move of the Month" feature. And yes, the stories (and pets within them) are often adorable. But entertainment is not the focal-point; usefulness is.

Farris's goal is to become easily discovered by prospects using search engines. But she's also focused on shepherding customers, offering them practical advice and giving them solutions to problems they can take action on. Yes, that advice draws on her target's emotions. That's why she showcases the joyful benefits of proper planning. But Farris tells stories with a specific purpose in mind. She's out to earn more. She wants customers' *behavior*.

Prompt an Action

PetRelocation.com's content marketing strategy is connected to a lead-management process. Being discovered by prospects is step 1. Getting them to take action—identify themselves as potential customers—is the key, and that means designing (planning) ways to prompt behavior (actions that signal what stage of the "relocation decision-making" process the prospect is in). For instance, alongside each blog story, Farris has placed three very clear calls to action, which are buttons that prompt customers to click. They are

1. I'm moving my pet **within the USA.**
2. I'm moving my pet **internationally.**
3. I have a **general inquiry.**

Clicking on each button brings targeted prospects to action-oriented landing pages. Domestic prospects are enticed to download MyPetRelocation, a free package that includes everything needed to relocate an animal easily and cost effectively. First name, last name, and e-mail address are collected. The company gives pet owners seven handy checklists, a free health certificate form and a Pet-Friendly Airport Report. For added incentive, the company includes a $100 discount coupon on any PetRelocation.com service.

International prospects land at a page offering a no-obligation consultation on their upcoming move. In exchange, they're asked to give PetRelocation.com their name, e-mail, telephone number, and basic profile information on their pet. Departure and destination information are also collected along with the estimated move date and reason for relocating. Qualitative information is also gathered on the prospect, such as what kind of special challenges they're facing and how soon they're expected to actually hire a pet relocation service (if hiring one at all).

Simply put, the company cannot afford to gain prospects' attention and hope for the phone to ring. That's why Farris works diligently to earn *insight* on her prospects' "state of need" in return for the valuable advice she provides. Of course, all of the information gleaned is automatically fed from the Web form into a lead-management/customer-relationship management software tool. The prospect enters a predefined courtship cycle involving e-mail and telephone follow-up. The business also uses marketing automation solution HubSpot to understand the source of leads. With a bit of elbow grease, Farris monitors conversion-to-sale ratios of each lead referrer from blog to Web site to Facebook and Twitter. This way, she knows who is performing best and is in a better position to optimize the return on investment.

Beyond keeping on top of practical metrics, Farris says helping a prospect feel like they *can* relocate their pet stress-free and safely is her primary goal. That's her hook: showing pet owners a compelling "emotional benefit" of a successful move. Deciding *if and when* the potential customer needs help from a capable, qualified business comes later. But it does come, and by design. That's why she's always prompting her prospects to act and connecting that behavior to a lead-management process aimed at converting prospects to customers.

Content marketing experts Anne Handley and C. C. Chapman provide practical advice in their book, *Content Rules*. "Share or solve, don't shill … show; don't just tell."

Much like PetRelocation.com's blog stories, Handley and Chapman say,

"Good content doesn't preach or hard-sell. Instead, it shows how your product lives in the world. It demonstrates … ."

PetRelocation.com is proving that content marketing can be smart and effective, but is it *really* profitable? For instance, by giving so much advice away, does a company risk chasing away paying customers? Does one risk "giving away the store?"

Shepherding Prospects

PetRelocation.com doesn't hesitate to give away their best tips and secrets. They recognize the mercenary truth: Almost everyone thinks they can relocate their pet, and Farris admits that most people can. Unfortunately, not everyone wants to pay for the convenience of her service, at least not in the early stages of consideration, when a pet owner's need is still forming. That's why PetRelocation.com is keen to educate their prospects—warm them up a bit and nurture them.

Here's another way of looking at it: by *shepherding* prospects, the company helps pet owners *guide themselves* toward—or away—from the company's services. Farris is letting prospects "self select" themselves as bonafide buyers. How? Through the process of learning about the *complexities* of pet relocation and reminding prospects of a successful move's *emotional* benefits.

Like many service businesses, PetRelocation.com is ultimately selling *trust and emotional relief.* Yes, they're providing tangible, functional value. But ultimately they're putting a price tag on peace of mind, and that's not something every pet owner is able to afford, as much as they'd like to.

Farris admits social media marketing isn't like eating pie all day long. She's constantly challenged, but not because she's giving away too much advice. In fact, she's attracting so many needy pet owners that "weeding the garden" is becoming more challenging. But Farris is excited at the chance to find better, faster ways to connect with the most needy, qualified customers. In a sea of tire-kickers, she's finding new ways to meet prospects that are most likely to purchase.

Make Lemonade

Founded in 2004 and now booking $4 million in revenue, PetRelocation.com is an innovator. The company isn't stopping at pioneering content marketing on the social Web. They're also finding ways to take "do-it-yourselfers" and generate new revenue. PetRelocation.com is being given a lot of lemons, and now they're making lemonade.

Giving practical answers to urgent questions using blogs and videos can get a business discovered, and it can earn potential customers' behavior in the form of a lead. But the practice also attracts "do-it-yourselfers"—prospects who will ultimately never buy, often because they cannot. In this way, PetRelocation.com is no different than any other business. Thus, the company is finding that being discovered is relatively easy, but connecting with people willing and able to pay for a service is crucial and a bit more challenging. Quickly identifying a poor lead and putting helpful information into their hands makes sense. But then again, PetRelocation.com has cooked up an even better approach to making content marketing pay.

Its downloadable MyPetRelocation tips package is changing—converting into a free matchmaking service for pet owners who want to relocate pets on their own. This innovative venture is giving pet owners who do *not* need PetRelocation.com's services the tools they *do* need to relocate pets themselves. For instance, the free service provides access to other like-minded, do-it-yourself pet owners though a digital community. This allows inexperienced pet owners to get tips and emotional support from seasoned veterans. The site also provides access to vetted service providers—many who already work with PetRelocation.com's service team.

PetRelocation.com is not only providing answers and tips to pet owners who do *not* want its service, it's monetizing them. The company has found a new revenue stream by focusing on "getting to no" faster with prospects—discovering what pet owners *do not want*. The company is now, itself, delicately moving into the lead generation business for its suppliers.

Similarly, River Pool and Spas's Marcus Sheridan is making hay out of leads outside his two-state territory. It didn't take long for him to realize the additional revenue stream he was sitting on. Today, he's selling excess leads (coming from outside his region) to out-of-state business owners and even manufacturers he represents.

"I didn't try to become the national fiberglass pool guru ... I don't seek these things, but they just happen if you produce content," says Sheridan, who is being flooded with e-mail requests for advice and on-site consultations across the country. His blog readers often insist on flying him in to oversee fiberglass pool installations. They're nervous about the quality and professionalism of the company they've hired. They trust him more.

"People tell me, 'You've taught me everything I know about fiberglass pools, and I have a few questions.' In fact, during the summer time I get a majority of e-mail inquiries from outside of Virginia and Maryland from people that just need help," says Sheridan.

This demand combined with another realization. "Right now, my blog is worth more than my entire company because of the value it has—the influence it has over the entire swimming pool industry," he says.

After entertaining a constant stream of inquiries from out-of-state buyers and manufacturers asking to buy his blog or joint venture with him, it became obvious: the blog was—like PetRelocation.com's blog—growing into a business itself.

"But it's all from this little guy in a town that only has a couple of stop lights. It's not supposed to work like that, but it does," says Sheridan, "simply because I was the first guy who wanted to talk about the industry—the good, the bad, and the ugly."

Sheridan says his decision to constantly address "the ugly" causes consumers to take a step back. People say, "Wow, this guy is the real deal." He says his candor causes respect levels to go through the roof.

"Because when you're brutally honest, customers know you're not invested in selling them junk, which is what they see with most Web sites. You know, the ones that are just glorified business cards and brochures that do nothing to *teach* customers. It really drives me nuts," says Sheridan, who's baffled as to why manufacturers aren't jumping into the educational, demand-generation pool.

But don't be fooled. Jenna White, Marcus Sheridan, and Rachel Farris aren't simply "being honest and transparent" with customers or simply listening to them. These savvy marketing pros are leveraging a proven *system*, a way to make social media sell off the hook.

Be a Thought Provoker, not Just a Thought Leader

"If you're using social media to show off what your business knows, you're limiting yourself to the tired, unsuccessful practice of traditional 'thought leadership,'" says Gunnar Branson, CEO of marketing and innovation consultancy Branson Powers (www.bransonpowers.com). Branson, like Marcus Sheridan, is reaping the benefits of *provoking* thought.

That said, Branson says he's been one of social media's biggest skeptics, having lived through VHS industrial videos, DVDs, and mini-DVDs that "basically got put on people's desks and never looked at before they ultimately got thrown away," he says with a smile.

"Whenever you hear lots of people talking about a great new way of selling … a great new way of marketing … there's a skeptic in me that goes, 'Okay, well, that's all fine-and-good, but at the end of the day, it's probably not going to do anything,'" says Branson. "But interestingly for me, social media keeps delivering business, and more than just interest or buzz—it just keeps delivering business.

And every time I think it won't, it does. It does for my clients and it does for me at a surprisingly consistent rate."

That's because Branson is *provoking reactions* with social media rather than positioning as a thought leader. He's finding new ways to generate something along the lines of a "hmmm … I never thought of that" from customers, all with generating leads in mind.

"The key is to discover what you're seeing that most people are not seeing right now," says Branson. "For instance, what might you know—right now— that's relatively *unknown and revealing*? Think in terms of a risk or opportunity that your listener, watcher, reader—ultimately customer—will react strongly to. Really strongly."

"Provoking 'hmms' from customers is important," says Branson.

"Because what you're trying to do is shift people into a mode of thought … give them a reason why they need to think about whatever-it-is in a powerful new way. And ultimately you must give them a reason to talk to you … so they can more clearly understand what you just provoked."

Branson's approach is powerful to business-to-business (B2B) professional services companies like insurance, legal, financial services, or consulting firms and manufacturers like medical device, pharmaceutical, industrial equipment, or computer networking suppliers, especially considering how ineffective the practice of being a thought leader has become.

"Many businesses try to establish themselves as thought leaders so people will come to them for advice, to help them solve problems," says Branson. "That makes sense. But unfortunately, most thought leadership efforts just confuse, frustrate, or bore people. For instance, businesses often write thick, white papers on an issue. Problem is, that issue is typically already well-known, and a survey of that issue is usually a summary of conventional thinking. By default, a white paper becomes a way to prove that you know the subject—just like the book reports we all did in school. After distributing it to as many people as possible, it comes as a surprise that no one actually reads it. Too often we end up valuing thought leadership by its weight, not by what's actually inside it. 'Oh, look how big it is, look how fine the typeface is, look how intelligent it seems to be.' Customers are rarely given new ideas that can help them do their jobs better."

Yes, Branson says social media is helping change that, but when customers are offered social media as another channel through which to receive "valuable information," they cut to the chase.

"Clients are saying, 'You know what, I'm going to the conferences and listening to your brilliant people talk; I get the white papers that I don't read; I get all this stuff from you, and the last thing I need is one more canned piece of communication. What I *really* want is what I get when I sit down with your people in person or even when I'm walking across town and getting an insight into something occurring in the market that I'm not already seeing. Tell me something that I don't know," says Branson, who is taking that simple idea and running with it along with his client, Jones Lang LaSalle (JLL), a global commercial real estate firm (www.joneslanglasalle.com).

"We took the idea (of telling clients something new) and asked ourselves, 'What if we were to create short videos that tee-up useful insights on the most important issues facing clients? What would happen?'"

"For instance, everything is 'going green' lately. Buildings are interested in conserving energy, getting green credits from local governments, et cetera. 'But wait—did you know that in the event of a storm, your building insurance designed to replace a typical tar roof won't cover the green landscaping or solar panels on your roof without specific changes in the contract?'"

Branson says this is just one example. There are plenty of bothersome problems plaguing JLL's customers. By focusing on urgent issues instead of promoting JLL's services, these videos prompt a steady stream of inquiries and leads, all through simple but provocative ninety-second videos. Sure, there needs to be truly valuable information within the media itself, and we'll discuss the precise formula in a later chapter. "But beyond offering useful information, the success of marketing should be about asking, 'How do I get customers to really need me, to be addicted to me ... so much so that they're ultimately willing to pay?'"

Branson and JLL are formatting the video clips in ways that do not provide free advice. Rather, "We're trying to create an irritation in clients. We're trying to get clients to think about something that maybe they didn't before. That's valuable, but it's not advice in terms of 'how are we going to fix this insurance problem?' Instead, it's 'here's a problem that you don't know you have.'"

"Actually, I think the success formula is incredibly close to the illegal narcotics trade," laughs Branson. "That is, you give someone a sample of a substance which gives them some degree of satisfaction but not enough for the desire to be completely sated. In other words, here, have a little bit of heroin. You will feel something that you will enjoy. But it won't be enough, and you'll want to have it again. So in order to have it again, you're going to have to talk to me, and you're going to have to buy some more heroin from me."

That's why today's true thought leaders are thought provokers. They're the people putting interesting, valuable, addictive thoughts "out there" in ways that prompt customers to ask for more, more often.

Practically speaking, Branson says it's the difference between talking about everything that you might know, who your clients are, or how great your products and services are, and talking about a particular change in the market lately—being honestly useful.

"To be effective, it should be presented as 'I've been talking with someone who's really smart that pointed out something that I'd never even thought about, and the more I think about it, the larger the implications appear.' That compels people to think, 'How can I get more of that kind of insightful information?' That leads them to reach out—to call you and ask for more. What a great way to start a sales call," says Branson, who gives simple, actionable tips on this B2B strategy in later chapters.

Selling HVAC Systems and Services with Facebook

The social Web sounds sexy, but finding customers, keeping them, trouncing the competition, and profiting are *still* what matters to companies like Logan Services. This small business isn't a dotcom "digital native." But the Dayton, Ohio-based heating, ventilating, and air conditioning business (HVAC) is generating a constant stream of local hardware and installation leads using Facebook and blogging.

"We're definitely not selling an impulse item," says Amanda Kinsella, the company's marketing director, who points out that most Facebook leads are unlike those coming from traditional, local advertising partners.

"When people find us on Facebook, it's not because they need our products or services. They need advice, and our job becomes one of shepherding them, leading them on a journey to discover that we have valuable solutions to their problems."

Kinsella started generating leads after sharing a few helpful blog stories on Facebook. Her update propagated across the company's Facebook network, which includes the regional Better Business Bureau and ServiceMagic.com, a marketing partner. Her status updates caught the interests of needy prospects inside her budding network, many of whom clicked to Logan Service's blog (www.logan-inc.com/blog-posts). There, prospects read helpful tips, saw clear calls to action in the sidebar of the blog page, and requested estimates—many of which converted to sales.

What does Kinsella blog about? Practical tips on what a home owner must do to qualify for a $1500 tax credit, for instance. Of course, earning credits has a lot to do with replacing old heating and air conditioning systems with higher efficiency models, and if customers need it, Kinsella's Web site offers quotations. It's this kind of helpful, compelling advice that Logan Services's customers *need* these days. Saving money through tax credits is what they're actively seeking. Helping customers save money in economically challenged times earns attention and trust and is occasionally producing sales.

"But be warned," says Kinsella. In social spaces like Facebook, being "liked" doesn't translate to an immediate customer need. In fact, research indicates Facebook "liking" doesn't translate to "permission to be marketed to" either, so hammering away with calls to action on Facebook isn't the answer. It takes a balanced approach.

For instance, Kinsella participates in (and prompts discussions about) "going green"—keying on courting customers with environmentally driven needs. She also generates quality leads by conversing with customers about saving money. She points out rebates from local utility companies, how to save on heating bills using whole-house humidifiers that "hold heat in" longer, how to reduce symptoms of allergies or asthma using whole-house air filters, and even retirement issues. Her intent is to foster *purpose-driven* relationships through sharing useful advice "so we can be there when prospects need our products and services," she says.

Kinsella's early Facebook experience inspired her to turn up the volume a bit, but in a very practical way. After all, she's a one-woman marketing operation.

The company agreed to give away a free Trane furnace on one condition: the company needed two hundred verifiable leads first. Once the designated number of contest participants was reached, it was "game on!" All participants needed to do was tell a compelling, personal story explaining why they need a new furnace.

In just two weeks, Kinsella walked away with nearly four hundred e-mail addresses from local prospects, most of whom will be needing a replacement furnace. Not bad compared to a prior TV- and Web site-based campaign. That effort netted a measly thirty-nine leads over four weeks. Logan Services's Facebook friend count also went from sixty-five to nearly four hundred in two weeks.

But wait. There's a bonus prize for Logan Services. Some contest participants ended up having a more urgent need. People who were really, truly needing a replacement furnace didn't take any chances. They signed up for the contest but also prepared for a possible loss. If they didn't win the free Trane system, they still needed a furnace. That's right, after entering, some contest applicants clicked through to Logan Services's Web site to get quotations.

Traditionally, Logan Services has relied on all the usual forms of advertising and marketing, ranging from TV ads and Yellow Pages listings to partnerships with big box retailers like Home Depot. They also set up booths at home improvement shows in shopping malls. Over the years, Kinsella says Logan Services has two kinds of prospects: those with urgent need and those with latent or "early-stage" need. But lately, using Facebook, she's beginning to tap into new kinds of leads.

"This has opened up a whole new category of people to talk to," says Kinsella. "Before social media, we were missing out on two different flavors of leads—people who don't know yet know they need us, and people who don't need us but know someone who does."

Kinsella, who grew up on a farm, calls what Logan Services is doing "referral farming," and she's been doing it at the company for a while now. Today, social media tools are breathing new life into the farming practice for Kinsella, who cringes at the thought of traditional brand advertising.

"To gain referrals, we cannot rely only on advertising," she says. "For our company, it's all done by word of mouth, so if I can get an extra boost to my referral farming using social media, I'm going to do it."

To the company's surprise, Facebook is supplying a steady stream of leads from their multi-state market. Logan Services *does* serve younger, first-time home buyers, but its sweet spot is the fifty-and-over crowd with an $80,000 or more household income, and that demographic is (surprisingly) *predominant* within the company's Facebook population.

But it's not all sunshine and lollipops, Kinsella warns. Sifting through the leads, qualifying them, and delicately following up on them requires skill, dedication, and patience. She is quick to point out that leads coming from social media typically require more nurturing. For instance, the Facebook giveaway contest resulted in many dozens of passion-filled short stories from people who *really* needed a new furnace. Following up with hundreds of prospects who did not win is an art form. In the end, she's converting many leads to lower-cost maintenance plans for existing systems. But Kinsella sees the time investment as worthwhile, given her ability to access new customer relationships.

"A conversation is all we need to begin our sales process. I think we've found a new hook on Facebook," says Kinsella, who sees the social Web as a chance to become an online advice center for residential heating and air conditioning.

If you think about it, Logan Services treats Facebook and blogs as an evolutionary next step, not a fundamental change in how business is done. Kinsella sees social media in a practical light and treats it accordingly. For instance, consider the idea of combining the lure of a free furnace system (a promotion) with time-tested direct response marketing techniques. That's not a new idea, but boosting it with a "group buying" incentive on Facebook was.

Logan Services is proof positive: Selling off the hook happens when businesses start putting more stock in *existing* knowledge and strengths and mixing in new tools.

Is This Revolution or Evolution?

I remember the first time I found myself at the mercy of technology. It was 1989, and personal computing was revolutionizing the world. I had so many questions. Everything seemed like a priority. I was a television production undergrad who took a high-paying, high-profile public relations internship at telecommunications goliath MCI. I was a fish out of water. I quickly found myself staring at a cubicle, a phone, a PC that looked more like a mini-SUV, and all kinds of networked applications. Yikes, where was the video equipment? I was lost, scared, and certain I wouldn't make it through my first week. I didn't have any of the answers about these new tools, and everything seemed like a priority.

Maybe you're dabbling in using the latest, most exciting social gizmos to market your business, like Twitter, Facebook, blogging, and LinkedIn. If you've got even a little bit of experience with them, you're probably asking smart questions.

- How many blog posts are needed to make the exercise effective?
- How much effort must be invested in Facebook to see a return?
- How can I manage my reputation among critics and enthusiast fans?
- How much Twitter engagement is needed to realize positive effect?
- How can I not "hard-sell" but still generate leads using LinkedIn?

I'd be surprised if one or two of these didn't sound familiar to you. They may even trigger an emotional response when you read them. Naturally, a lot of business folks I meet are stressing out over these questions. That's because answering and prioritizing them is daunting for most of us. Sometimes it feels like social media tools are beyond our abilities. Sure, social media marketing is "a must," but it's tricky, filled with new rules and strange words, not to mention tips and advice. There's no shortage of the stuff! Everyone is busy saying that everything is a priority.

But are you really lost, or are you just *convinced* you're without a map? Let's consider *where* your priorities are coming from. For instance, why are "managing your online reputation" and "developing enthusiasts" more important than generating sales? Because a company selling social "buzz monitoring" software says so? Why is the end goal for Twitter something called engagement? Because someone who wrote a book on Twitter decided so? Who said you cannot use LinkedIn to generate sales leads? Research funded by an agency selling traditional advertising?

Chris Kenton, CEO of data intelligence company SocialRep, once said to me, "Ever notice how the people who are the most lost are the most confident in telling others how to find the way?"

It's not your imagination. These "must do's" are often being birthed by gurus, consultants, and software companies who are well-intentioned. But they have something to sell you, and sometimes they can misguide you.

Be transparent, be authentic, be "human," and always listen. We are incessantly told these ideas are what companies must do with social media immediately. They seem to make sense, and that's why most businesses are focusing on them. But how practical are ideas like making your businesses "more human" as compared to "more focused on sales?" Haven't you always participated in conversations with customers?

Have you ever felt like you're being *sold* answers that don't connect to your questions?

The Right Coach

I remember freaking out at my desk during my first day at MCI. The tools surrounding me were completely foreign. I started asking myself rapid-fire questions. "What are all these software tools, and how will I learn to use all of them in the right way?" And on and on. I convinced myself that the tools staring me in the face were technically beyond me and that prioritizing them and my work would require superhero powers.

My boss saw how panic stricken I was. Doug was a true mentor. He sat me down and showed me something. That is, how to stop worrying about the tools. "Just take a deep breath ... let me show you how these things work," Doug said. Afterward, I was promptly issued a long list of projects. Heh. I was thrown into the fire!

But suddenly I had all the answers. I dug in. I selectively applied my new tools to the tasks at hand. Writing press releases, pitching stories, effectively dealing with uninterested and verbally abusive editors, and managing crisis communications situations. Sure enough, I *already knew* how to do what needed to be done and how to do it. I also knew how to prioritize my new tasks. I merely needed to take a breath, consider how to apply the new tools, and get to work. I needed a bit of confidence in what I *already knew how to do*. That was the key to success.

I climbed a seemingly insurmountable mountain by focusing on making new tech tools produce outcomes. E-mail, word processing, and clunky tools like Lotus Notes weren't that scary after all because I already knew how to make the *truly important things* happen—tasks like writing effective press releases, responding to media inquiries, and getting employee newsletters written and delivered. I succeeded because I never lost track of the end goal and because I had *a good guide*, the right coach: a true, credentialed expert who had *my interests* in mind, a coach who was *invested* in my success. He was someone who focused me on outcomes—the task at hand. *My* task at hand. Which, of course, happened to be his, too.

And that's why I've written this book. To guide you toward the outcomes you need.

We'll come back to addressing all the usual social media questions most businesses worry about throughout the book. And as you read on, keep in mind

1. *Where* your most urgent concerns come from
2. How worrying about them may not be serving *your* interests
3. How focusing on the *tactical* application of tools like Twitter and Facebook may actually be getting in your way of selling with them.

CHAPTER 2

DESIGN TO SELL

*"Social behavior in humans is as old as our species,
so the emergence of an Internet based on social behavior
is simply our rudimentary technology catching
up with offline life. Thinking about 'social design'
should be embedded in everything we do,
and not thought of in isolation."*

*Paul Adams
Global brand experience manager, Facebook*

CONSIDER the five businesses we just met. The opportunity is clear: to design digital conversations in ways that produce meaningful, relevant, value-laden experiences for customers and profits for your business.

But might the answer to selling more with social tools be rooted in starting conversations that are worth having and knowing whom to converse with? Might it be more powerful to converse in ways that generate customer inquiries and questions you can help them solve?

These ideas have always been the secret to success since man invented the idea of commerce itself. So, could asking these questions of ourselves lead to practical, actionable answers? Could the difference between selling off the hook or not be, at the core, asking better questions? Gunnar Branson of Branson Powers says yes.

"The fastest way to get on the right track is to ask yourself, 'What is it about what we're doing that's unique … what is it about us that is addictive, that people want more of?'" says Branson.

Branson says that once you've answered that question, *then* it's time to ask, "How do we give customers a free sample of it?"

From a tactical standpoint, Twitter, Facebook, LinkedIn, blogging, and YouTube aren't that much different from direct mail, publishing, e-mail, or brochures, according to Branson. They're not different in terms of the practical part. They're distribution methods. And yes, they're better. In fact, our new technical tools are a better way to leverage networks of people by making the network itself more tangible.

But Branson says the same fundamentals that made communication powerful thousands of years ago are still at work today; the same thing that spurred people to action then are what work today.

"The reasons why people say, 'Hey, let's go *do* something—let's *buy* something or let's follow this leader'—are the same. The kinds of communications that work have been around as long as human beings have collected together. The skills we need to create buying behavior aren't changing. Social media simply makes us able to deliver communications at a scaled level very quickly. But that does not mean we suddenly forget everything we know about how to persuade or lead people."

"We have to use those same skills," says Branson. "We have to inject them into this new environment. And unless you are a celebrity, you're not going to build a successful business by merely being entertaining like Ashton Kutcher. Yes, he's managed to get millions of people to follow him on Twitter, but I don't know if that could lead to the sale of anything other than the entertainment value of Ashton Kutcher. Non-entertainment companies probably wouldn't benefit from following that model."

Beyond Attention Lie Sales

Businesses that sell off the hook with social media are reaching beyond attracting customers or even coercing them to prefer a brand. They're focusing on discovering and capturing sales using two practical success principles:

1. *Design* to create a constant stream of behavior.
2. *Publish* useful, relevant tools and services that solve problems.

Consider your current social media activities: everything you're doing to "join the conversation." You're tweeting, blogging, and posting updates on Facebook. Is what you're doing talking with or talking "at" customers? Are you interacting with them? Keep these questions in the back of your mind as this chapter unfolds. We'll return to them soon.

Let's discover how successful businesses are making every social media encounter produce *behavior*—acts that ultimately induce sales. Let's learn how they're guiding empowered customers toward destinations they (customers) choose—ultimately arriving at products and services—and let's witness how offering tools and information to customers makes it easy to prompt leads and sales.

I promise: the success formula will come into clear focus. For instance, we'll contrast approaches taken by companies like Wisconsin-based Anchor-Bank with global financial goliath Chase, among others. You'll see how some businesses are making this formula work, all while others limit themselves to fun-and-games on Facebook.

In the end it's all about nurturing *behavior*: actions that foster demand.

Driving In-store Sales with Facebook

In 2009, Burger King decided it was time to drive customers into stores using Facebook. The fast food franchise would use a discount coupon to create incentive, but the idea reached beyond luring hungry Facebook users with free hamburgers. In the end, results were impressive. The company delighted customers by improving their overall Facebook experience, tracked its financial return on investment, and optimized for profit along the way.

Burger King wisely realized most Facebook users have a problem. It's one that you may have. Most of us have "friends" who aren't *really* friends. They're people we've rather blindly (or out of curiosity) agreed to be Facebook friends with. Burger King figured a good number of Facebook users would like to clean house—purge their "non-friend" friends. This would improve their daily experience using Facebook by decreasing irrelevant "noise" from unwanted friends.

Think about your own Facebook experience. You probably have Friends who you'd rather not have cluttering up valuable space. Of course, you can "clean house" immediately if you want to invest the time, but most of us don't have any real incentive to selectively purge unwanted Facebook friends, even if it means improving our Facebook experience.

So Burger King teamed up with digital agency Refresh Partners to develop the Whopper Sacrifice campaign and give Facebook users that incentive. Burger King created a way for people to improve their Facebook experience and be rewarded for doing so. The company created a value-laden utility in the form of an application and then *published* it to burger-loving Facebook users on Facebook's platform.

Through a simple Facebook widget application, the "sacrifice" allowed Facebook users to clean house—to take action not to simply view, see, or hear an advertising message, but to *behave*. People began "unfriending" undesired friends from Facebook accounts—sacrificing them—all for the opportunity to win a free Whopper sandwich. All hungry users needed to do was unfriend a designated number of unwanted friends. Doing so brought them to a printable coupon Web page, no strings attached. The campaign was a huge success, with hundreds of thousands of "unwanted friend" relationships ending in just a few weeks time.

At first glance this looks like a simple coupon promotion. But considering the layers of value—experienced by *both* Burger King and customers—this campaign was groundbreaking. Burger King customers were given incentive to do something they *already wanted* to do—improve their Facebook experience. Burger King didn't need to convince customers to do anything they didn't already want to do. In fact, Burger King agreed to bonus everyone who performed the act with a free premium sandwich. It was a win-win for customers.

On the flip side, Burger King was able to use a cutting-edge social network to drive customers into its restaurants. Burger King focused on creating demand. In fact, it could track a handful of business metrics (coupon redemption, up-sell take rate, non-usage, and attempts to use a coupon outside of the redemption period) to prove return on investment.

In this scenario, actual profit of the campaign can be tracked, and Burger King can optimize the campaign to create more sales, more often. For instance, the redemption period can be tweaked. Studying redemption patterns may reveal that customers need more time to use the coupon, for instance. Maybe limits set on the "deal-earning behavior" can be adjusted upward or downward in a way that creates more redeemed coupons and sales. In other words, unfriending at the rate of "one coupon per eight unfriends" might drive more sales than "one coupon per fifteen actions."

In the end, the Whopper Sacrifice was a marvelous "digital direct response" marketing success for Burger King. There was one problem: it was frowned upon by Facebook. The tremendous benefits to Facebook users and Burger King came at the expense of the social networking giant. You see, Burger King provided its members with double-layers of value without Facebook seeing a dime. Customers got a free burger and a qualitatively better Facebook experience. Burger King was able to create demand, track its return on investment, and optimize campaign performance. But most of Facebook's value is rooted in an ability to generate money using banner ads—a *quantitative* game. Facebook's current value is based on the number of users and "friend" relationships. So, the rapidly spreading "unfriending" activity was destructive to Facebook's core economics—the very heartbeat of its revenue system.

Although this campaign was short-lived, it was groundbreaking. It used Facebook to drive customers into restaurants and captured sales, and it used the two key success principles. It prompted customer *behavior* by focusing on what customers' truly *needed* beyond a fast meal, *and* Burger King made itself *useful* to Facebook-addicted customers—again, in a way that went beyond selling food. It catered to a need and published an interactive tool, a device that allowed customers to do what they already wanted to do—that is, have a better Facebook experience.

Burger King successfully motivated *behavior* among customers in ways that aligned directly with Burger King's goal: to sell. Contrast Burger King's approach with American Airlines' "NYC Challenge 10,000" campaign. American offered anyone who would "friend" them on Facebook access to special promotions. But beyond offering discounts, the campaign was not designed to provide a useful outcome to fliers or the company. American simply handed out coupons, and customer behavior was limited to spreading the word about the campaign to friends.

American was so eager to do something on Facebook that it made a common mistake. First, the company got caught up in the idea of gaining attention through "friending" activity. The airline was focused on behavior but with a very limited outcome in mind. The need American catered to wasn't anything more than customers seeking discounts. It wasn't a uniquely compelling need, and the promotion itself had limited usefulness to fliers.

Could American have done better? For instance, consider its long-standing frequent flier program—a seriously useful tool to the company and fliers. Also targeted to deal-oriented, value-conscious fliers, the frequent flier program keeps customers flying and assigning value to doing so with American. Fliers constantly feel like they're earning value, and American keeps prompting them to make more purchases. The program drives behavior.

But here's where American's frequent flier program is different from this Facebook promotion. American's program is designed in a way to keep specific, identifiable customers flying. The frequent flier program itself has intrinsic value; it's something that American can use again and again to keep fliers flying. In contrast, this Facebook promotion handed out discounts to, relatively speaking, strangers, all in hopes of fliers redeeming them and spreading them among other friends. But these kinds of Facebook programs are not able to keep customers flying as well as a frequent flier program. For instance, American owns and operates a database marketing engine that powers its frequent flier program. In contrast, functionally speaking, Facebook does not have the ability to deliver a similar toolkit to American.

In its rush into social media marketing, American's "NYC Challenge

10,000" campaign didn't create value for fliers beyond discounts, and neither did it create a useful marketing asset for American. Facebook's platform wasn't designed to help American keep customers in the air. What the airline ended up "buying" through its Facebook campaign was an expensive, anonymous group of deal-seekers, not an active database of brand loyalists. By relying on Facebook "friending," American lost the ability to leverage behavior into more flying activity.

Consider our two success principles. American prompted customer *behavior* by focusing on what fliers *needed* but not in ways beyond its own product. It limited its usefulness to "cheaper" in a market where price is a commodity, a weak competitive tool. It published discounts rather than a *useful* tool that provided new, valuable benefits. American's design was relatively poor.

Increase Share of Customer Wallet with Content Marketing

Banking is a tough business, but despite increased regulation and skeptical customers, Wisconsin-based AnchorBank (www.anchorbank.com) is increasing what banks call "share-of-wallet." That is, the percentage ("share") of a customer's expenses ("of wallet") that AnchorBank's products and services have earned. At the same time, AnchorBank is boosting referrals and leads. They're bucking the trend among banks because they're thinking differently about social media marketing—in ways that produce more profitable ways of doing it. Anchor Bank has a different perspective on social media in general: a sensible, practical one.

Unlike its competitors, this financial services company is using social media to make its products benefits real, tangible when and where customers express a need that relates to them, even if that need is in a latent stage. The bank is educating needy customers using content delivered via the Web and in retail branches. But more importantly, AnchorBank is listening and *responding* in ways that prompt customers to take action—to do what they're quite inclined to do—that is, get involved in the process of buying a product or service.

One might think the educational content AnchorBank produces is the key. But it's not. It's a necessary tool. What powers their success is a process that starts with listening, shifts to responding (distributing information), and then follows up with prospects. Let's take a closer look at how AnchorBank is making content marketing grow their business.

Good Advice Is Never Truly Free

AnchorBank's challenge was like most banks'. In fact, it was like most service-based businesses. More and more, customers need help making complex decisions. Nearly everyone these days expects valuable advice to come at little (if any) cost. Think about your own financial life. It could be making a decision on college savings plans, retirement savings tools, starting up a small business, bracing for a divorce or getting married. Again, probably like your business, most of AnchorBank's customers demand an increasing amount of trusted advice for free.

The good news is AnchorBank has the expertise to guide them, but the bank's target market wasn't turning to banks for advice out of habit. Think about how you view banks in your life. We tend to use them as vaults, places to make routine transactions. We don't really turn to banks for advice on pressing personal or business finance needs. We usually tap personal relationships, professional financial advisers, celebrity advisers like Suze Orman, or free online resources like BankRate.com.

"Banks are seen too narrowly as the place to go for deposits and loans, a place to go to transact," says Stewart Rose, CEO of financial marketing agency Truebridge Inc. (www.truebridge.com). "That's fine if a bank is comfortable with a small share of their customer's wallet."

But AnchorBank certainly is not, so its solution is practical and effective. Guided by Rose's company, they're publishing and distributing easy-to-read guidebooks. The bank is giving impulsive, emotionally driven banking customers *useful* information that they need. Maybe it's tips on lowering personal debt or finding better ways of controlling spending. Probably like your business, AnchorBank's expertise spans a wide variety of customer needs. So it makes sense for them to give useful advice to customers in digital and physical guidebook formats.

But here's where it gets powerful. This content marketing strategy is supported by a behavior-driven framework—a system of prompts that leads customers toward the purchase of products they need. Again, customers expect consulting and advice for free, and AnchorBank obliges, but not without expectation of the consumer. The bank *learns* from them. It "listens" using the Web and branch staff. But it also "logs" or databases what it hears. This part is key because the bank is building *process* around distribution (and use) of its print and Web content.

In effect, AnchorBank's educational system is helping customers identify themselves as candidates for products they're becoming increasingly inclined to buy.

Trade Knowledge for Insights

AnchorBank isn't just publishing useful knowledge; it's also discovering customers' needs, generating leads, and managing them. Think of this "useful financial advice distribution system" as a chain of non-monetary *exchanges* with customers.

"Most people measure conversion-to-sale by the ultimate action they want users to take," says author, speaker, and sales conversion expert Bryan Eisenberg. "For instance, how many people bought, subscribed, or registered. But each of these actions comprises a series of smaller actions."

Eisenberg says each of these micro-actions—or omission of one—is a step closer or further away from AnchorBank's ultimate objective. "Micro-actions," he says, "are the measures of 'almost success.'" But they serve an important purpose: to nurture business leads along.

That's why AnchorBank's content marketing program always *exchanges* information with customers. Customers trade insight on what they need in return for advice. That's the hook. The way they express need may be explicit or implicit, urgent or latent. For instance, access to documents inside Anchor-Bank's Financial Answer Center (www.financialinformationcenter.anchorbank. com) is given in exchange for a customer's e-mail address. The bank provides publications focusing on a variety of topics. Hence, any given customer's need (general intent) can be easily derived from the request itself. Sometimes the bank asks for a bit of additional, qualitative information on *why* the customer needs the information they're requesting.

Let's say a customer requests tips on how to buy a home for the first time. This customer gets categorized by AnchorBank as a first-time mortgage candidate. Follow up from a qualified mortgage banker is scheduled to nurture and close the lead. If a request comes in via the physical branch, it's associated with the customer's account—likewise when the exchange happens via the Web.

Whether the customer is online at AnchorBank.com or in a retail branch, the bank is nurturing referrals and leads using physical documents or electronic PDFs. Within these documents customers find information that solves problems. Of course, the bank is marketing to customers, often pushing their buttons by pumping up the emotional end benefit of a product. That part doesn't change. And yes, AnchorBank's overall online strategy is focused on earning (and maintaining) customers' trust through a "human touch," but it's also designed to net the bank business leads, opportunities to cross-sell products in ways that leverage that trust. In fact, customers appreciate the opportunity to learn about relevant products by having them presented as answers to their problems.

Show, Don't Tell

In life, most of us don't plan. We react, especially with our finances, and we don't usually turn to banks for advice on complex decisions. So most banks (like most businesses) try to change their image. They *tell* us how they really *do* care or *do* have answers. But AnchorBank takes a different approach: *giving* customers answers they need. AnchorBank is making its product's benefits real when and where customers display a need for them. This bank is *showing* customers that it's different, not merely telling them. But they're not giving away the store so much as they're giving customers a chance to signal what they need help with. Showing customers you have answers they need works better than telling them.

What sets AnchorBank apart is how, when, and where tools get distributed, not the informational tools or content itself.

For instance, think about your last physical visit to your bank. Maybe you popped in to make a routine deposit. When entering the branch or teller window, one typically sees and hears about one thing: rates. Think about the promotional signage you see inside most banks. Again, they're mostly pushing rates. Unfortunately for banks, this is how customers interact with them. We walk in to make a transaction and then get out. Most often, we're not looking to solve a problem, although we often have a good handful!

But what if your bank presented solutions to your problems? At AnchorBank, customers frequently see and hear answers to a variety of life's problems. That makes customers more aware that AnchorBank has those answers. Customers are regularly *prompted* to chat about major life events with branch employees, and that's resulting in more customers *experiencing* the answers: receiving the guide books not only in the branch, but on AnchorBank's Web site and through social media. This bank *shows* customers the answers by actually delivering the advice.

Think Like a Designer, Not an Advertiser

In many ways, AnchorBank is using its valuable knowledge just as an industrial designer uses ergonomics. They're giving customers a free value-added educational service that conforms to where, when, and how they want their problem solved. Think of it as "form factors" of information consumption. Some banking customers may display a latent, early-stage need while casually interacting with a bank teller. Others may do the same while logging in to check their statement online or pay a bill. AnchorBank is always there eliciting a response from customers, and that response is part of a traditional lead-management process.

What sets AnchorBank apart from other financial services firms is *how, when, and where tools get distributed*, not the informational tools or content itself. The secret is the process design that makes marketing functional. AnchorBank is prompting customers to express need, nurturing it, and ultimately capturing sales: increasing share-of-wallet.

Improving on Process

Acquiring new accounts is just as important as growing share-of-wallet of existing customers, and that was Chase's focus with its Plus One Facebook campaign aimed at students. But students actually needing Chase's card were never given an opportunity to move toward it. Chase failed to give students answers, tools that improved their ability to manage finances, for instance. Therefore, Chase didn't gain new, first-time credit card customers using social media. Chase prompted students to express themselves but not in ways that ultimately signed them up for a credit product, a tool they probably needed. Let's learn what went wrong and how Chase could have improved the outcome.

The goal of Chase's multi-faceted Plus One marketing campaign was to enroll student card holders. To crate awareness for its Facebook element, the bank invested in banner ads. The banners invited students to join a Facebook group page. The group was designed for students who wanted to learn about the new Plus One credit card product designed to meet their unique needs.

Chase also offered group members the chance to earn redeemable points. This created an incentive for getting students to join the group. When group members spread the word about the Plus One card, they earned points. In the end, points could be "cashed-in" for DVDs and other merchandise students typically want. Student organizations also earned points for each referred student who became a Facebook group member. About 34,000 students participated in the initial campaign.

Unfortunately, Chase's Facebook group had no means to listen for or capture information on students' actual state of need. For instance, did the students Chase attracted need a card? If so, what credit line and services did they expect? When might they need one? What was their level of credit savvy? The bank communicated with Plus One group members without much rhyme or reason about once a month or so, and it used Facebook to deliver announcements about the product. Essentially, the bank advertised rather than educate students on getting the most from credit cards.

Chase failed to leverage "what mattered" most to students, making it nearly impossible to prompt them to apply for its card in a social environment. For instance, the bank didn't design a *process* that hooked and followed up with students. In effect, Chase didn't generate applications on leads that could be pursued and closed.

Yet the program itself was heralded by the bank's team as a win based on the number of fans generated and the involvement of several hundred student "ambassadors" who weighed in. These students gave feedback on how the Facebook program was designed, but this kind of listening merely amounts to a digital focus group—market research, not a sales-focused process.

Paul Adams, Facebook's global brand experience manager, puts it very bluntly when he says, "We're still seeing the fans and followers arms race—businesses trying to gather as many fans as possible. But I think that's fundamentally wrong."

When asked if there is too much focus on the total number of Twitter followers, friends, or Facebook "likes," he is equally blunt.

"Many brands run competitions on social media platforms. You have to 'like' or 'follow' that business to enter. So the question is whether they are making connections with advocates of their brand or with people who simply love competitions. If it's the latter, then they're filling their social media interactions and data with noise," says Adams, who says *behavior* is at the center of successful social strategy.

Using behavior to sell off the hook takes planning and the proper tool set. For instance, prompting students to give insight on their needs and level of credit savvy would have allowed Chase to actively market the Plus One card to students more effectively. Doing so would have allowed the bank to take follow-up actions and move students toward applications.

As another example, Chase provided CDs and other prizes students crave as an incentive to spread the word. But what if Chase had provided students with *useful* information on first-time home buying, small business loans, maximizing credit, or avoiding the "debt trap?" What if the incentive to take action was useful information that students *really needed*, rather than everyday trinkets? Chase could have designed its Plus One Facebook campaign in a way that discovered specific needs of individual (or groups of) students. In other words, they could have identified students who needed the card immediately. Likewise, Chase could have set up a lead-nurturing e-mail or direct mail marketing routine for students who expressed need in twelve months or more. To accomplish this, the bank's team could have made use of known *behavior* patterns of students based on typical needs.

For instance, students often use Facebook to share trivial tidbits, but they use it to share useful information, too. A simple budgeting tool (application) has tremendous usefulness for most students, as would a widget providing daily tips on saving money or managing credit. By providing these kinds of tools within Facebook, Chase could have prompted students to express need *and* invented ways to induce behavior. Chase could have created reasons to interact directly with students who truly needed the Plus One credit card.

Specifically, Chase's Plus One Facebook campaign could have given students a tool that helped them solve important problems—like managing finances—in ways that ultimately prompted Plus One card applications. Rather than earning students' feedback on their campaign's structure, Chase could have earned students' questions to which their card ultimately provides answers.

Netting Leads with Multimedia, Microsites, and Viral E-mail

Sometimes businesses are forced to expand and grow customers outside of a traditional demographic. Like many of their competitors, Australia-based Queensland Teachers Credit Union (QTCU) ended up reaching outside its core market: teachers. Quite suddenly, retaining its most important customers became vital to the company's survival. Like most businesses do, the company hatched a novel ad campaign hoping to win back the hearts and minds of their most important customer group. But thanks to a smarter-than-usual social marketing approach, the 2009 ad campaign quickly turned into a lead generation gold mine. The results: 1,025 schools got involved to generate 14,000 opt-in e-mail subscribers. It created a database of prospects complete with name, age, occupation, postal code, and product holdings. Of course, this didn't happen by accident. Like Burger King, QTCU focused on *behavioral design* and a clever mix of very practical Web marketing tools.

In an interview with TheFinancialBrand.com, QTCU's Chris Moses said the credit union was looking to rekindle the relationship with its historical base: teachers. Because the demand among members for loans was outstripping deposit growth, QTCU needed more deposits (cash) to service customers. But a good number of teachers resented the expansion beyond QTCU's roots in education. They weren't interested in opening deposit accounts with QTCU; they no longer saw the advantage and felt betrayed.

"The campaign was about giving something back to our original core audience: teachers," Moses said. At that moment, teachers were in the middle of enterprise bargaining over pay disputes. QTCU designed a bold concept to tap into the sentiment teachers were expressing. The business decided to focus on indulging teachers.

Other than a pay raise, there are few things teachers want more than a better, more comfortable work environment, so QTCU would give a single school the chance to win the *ultimate* staffroom through a $30,000 "staffroom makeover." The bait was tempting, but just as Burger King understood, QTCU realized its campaign would generate a bigger sales prospecting list if it was designed to let teachers "do what they're naturally inclined to do." QTCU's idea was to help teachers earn the *recognition and affirmation* they craved, and that's exactly what they did. The campaign encouraged teachers to foster social recognition among people most important to them. Winning the staffroom makeover meant teachers needed to earn the votes of their supporters.

Teachers are busy, time-stretched people, just like most customers are, and getting their attention was step 1. So the credit union's ad agency invented a school in sunny California with an *amazing* staffroom. Actually, it was quite obscene. This staffroom was over-the-top, beyond plush. The world-class room included a private billiards hall, gleaming kitchen and lunch areas, plunge pool and hot tub spa, designer bathrooms, a giant salt water aquarium with over fifty reef fish, and more. This make-believe staffroom became "real" through the magic of a low-cost, practical PowerPoint show featuring photographs and brief descriptions.

QTCU released the short "Amazing Teacher Staffrooms" Powerpoint show to a targeted group of teachers as an e-mail attachment. Subject line: "You've got to see this." The plan was to encourage teachers to share this dream staffroom with colleagues, and share they did. The PowerPoint went viral, and teachers were able to indulge in a bit of humor. A call to action at the end of the show said, "Pass this on to your principal; you never know your luck!"

At the most simplistic level, QTCU prompted behavior: a bit of laughter and sharing. But it also tapped into the emotional state of teachers. At the time it was volatile. If you think about it, the company's gesture (offering images of a dream staffroom) was very much about giving teachers hope. But more importantly, this was an "emotional foundation" being laid. QTCU was setting up to deliver on a more potent, behavior-driven phase.

One week later, the credit union followed-up with "Staffroom for Improvement"—the chance for teachers to win a $30,000 makeover for their staffroom.

Posters were sent to schools all over Queensland, directing them to a competition microsite. Here, teachers were treated to photos of what really, truly could be theirs: a "tricked out" staff room. Upon landing on the site, a stale, old staff room gets updated within a few seconds. Images of the updated room were designed to appeal to men and women. A clear call to action appeared at the bottom of the Web page: "Win the ultimate staffroom."

To qualify and participate, schools simply filled out a form. They provided a bit of information about themselves. In just two weeks, 1,025 of Queensland's 1,700 schools bit the hook: they registered to participate. Schools then competed head to head. Using everything in their power, teachers mustered up votes. From Facebook to e-mail newsletters to print newsletters to huge signs on school's frontages, schools did everything in their power to get the vote out for teachers. Over 1 million Queenslanders were estimated to have heard of the competition, mostly through teachers themselves.

In 2009, QTCU collected e-mail addresses to keep 32,000 voters and teachers up to date on vote count during the 18-day contest. In the end, schools generated 14,000 opt-in e-mail subscribers. This valuable prospecting database included customers' (and potential customers') names, ages, occupations, postal codes, and product holdings. Even more exciting, this database became the backbone for 2010's promotion, which produced 60,000 votes for 1,200 schools. QTCU was able to grow the leads database by 18,000 for a grand total of 32,000 sales prospects in 2010.

Sure, the 2,700 Facebook fans and TV, radio, and newspaper media buzz were also noteworthy, but considering QTCU struggled (over a few years' time) to grow its database of prospects to just 1,500, the 32,000 new leads trumped fandom and buzz.

The Staffroom for Improvement campaign worked because, like Burger King's Whopper Sacrifice, it had multiple layers of incentives for the target audience and a meaningful output for the business sponsoring it: leads. It had a worthwhile, valuable prize that motivated teachers. The promise was simple: "win the ultimate staffroom." But it also had a voting element that keyed on recognition, one of life's most basic, instinctual social needs. Tens of thousands of votes were cast for teachers by their peers, students, families, and community members. It was a true, grassroots groundswell of *purposeful* behavior.

> *The campaign worked—it generated attention, engagement and increased positive sentiment among teachers. But it also captured sales leads by creating behavior.*

Obviously teachers want a nicer—if not plush—working environment. But this campaign *also* focused on what teachers are naturally inclined to take action on. Is it difficult to motivate someone—anyone, really—to be recognized and affirmed? I can think of far more challenging tasks, and mixing the request with an incentive (a good, old-fashioned sweepstakes) isn't rocket science. These ideas have always worked. They just beg to be supercharged through the use of Web and social media tools.

Again, the Staffroom for Improvement campaign worked on the business side. Yes, it generated attention, engagement, and positive sentiment among teachers. It got teachers to feel better about the credit union. It also created a deeper sense of trust and respect for the QTCU. But it also captured sales leads, all by focusing socially driven *behavior* that made teachers feel good about themselves. But success was based on what teachers physically acted on. This campaign was something you actually did. It used a *publishing* approach to get the job done, combining e-mail, a Web site (www.qtcu.com.au), and multimedia (PowerPoint, of all things).

Make Sales with Education

HubSpot serves customers that are probably a lot like you. They're hungry online marketers of business-to-business and business-to-consumer goods and services. These everyday business folk need a better way to manage leads, and HubSpot sells a suite of software tools that help do exactly that.

As a way to create sales leads for itself, HubSpot offers various "toolboxes" that solve common problems. These are addictive, easy-to-use, educational utilities, really neat solutions that empower customers with knowledge—practical information they can use immediately. For instance, HubSpot's free Web site grader tool (www.grader.com) allows a business owner to instantly understand how well their Web site stacks up against others. The grader passes critical judgment on criteria like how many inbound links are coming into the site or how many of the site's pages Google has included in its index. But HubSpot's tool wisely scores qualitative Web site aspects, too. It gives valuable, *actionable* feedback to site owners on things like readability level: "Is your Web site content understandable, and to whom?" The free Web site grader tool also provides a Web image summary: "Are images discoverable by search engines and tagged properly?"

The automated diagnostic tool even looks for a conversion form, telling HubSpot's prospect if their Web site has a good, reliable means to generate leads at the moment. The best part of all is that the Web site grader's scores are designed to induce *more* questions and expressions of need from the user. Yup. It's designed to help customers self-select themselves as business leads for HubSpot's software product.

For instance, the Web site grader may find no means to generate leads on a prospect's Web site. Not good. So if you think about it, the next question a user will likely ask is, "What would it take to change that?" HubSpot stands ready with an easy-to-see call to action promoting a free trial of their software. Genius. But what if the Web site grader *does* find a Web form (collecting lead data) on the prospect's Web site? The obvious question becomes, "Is there a way to *improve* my Web site's form: make it collect more qualified leads, more often?" Yup. You guessed it. HubSpot stands ready again with a call to action for its product that scratches that itch.

But let's say the person using HubSpot's Grader is researching a competitive Web site, not their own. Sure enough, the tool is designed to be useful to the user *and* HubSpot because answers spawned by HubSpot's tool are always designed to elicit *more questions* from users—questions that can be answered by the company's products.

But here's where it gets really good. Maybe the prospect is not yet ready to buy or take a free test drive of HubSpot's paid software solution. No problem. The company offers more free, educational options, including Inbound Marketing University (IMU). Prospects' burning questions can almost certainly be answered by HubSpot's full-blown online marketing educational resource. And—you guessed it—this entity serves as a lead-generation program for HubSpot, too. The

IMU (www.inboundmarketing.com/university) is just another means to continually *prompt and capture expression of need* from customers: it's a hook.

Not all users of HubSpot's free tools find themselves immediately ready for one of their software products, but most *are* needing what the company's free IMU offers. That's why HubSpot offers this *no-cost* means to improve its prospects' *Web marketing skills*. We'll discuss this lead-generating powerhouse in more detail in chapters ahead.

HubSpot is "proving out" our success principles, too. It's publishing an extensive array of free, *useful* Web-based tools and generating leads for itself. Like the other success stories we've profiled, everything HubSpot does online elicits *behavior* from prospects. Through its free tools, the company is constantly soliciting, storing, and occasionally acting on various expressions of customers' needs. It's a process. HubSpot isn't just giving help away to "engage." Neither is the company wanting to keep customers on their Web site longer or remind prospects of their existence. Everything they're doing is aimed at increasing sales.

A Better Approach

Can your business experience this kind of success selling using social media? Most businesses can if they adjust their *expectations* of social media marketing and improve the questions they're asking about it.

"*The thing* (social media) has, in many instances, replaced the *why*," says BrandBuilder Marketing's Olivier Blanchard (www.thebrandbuildermarketing .com).

"Instead of hearing executives ask, 'Can we use social media to sell, improve customer service, or to recruit better candidates,' I most often hear, 'What should our social media strategy focus on?' Or, 'Okay, we have a Facebook page and a Twitter account. Now what?'"

"And that's the wrong approach," says Blanchard. A traditional, well-founded approach to social media application looks like this:

Business problem → business strategy to solve the problem
→ incorporate social media into said business strategy.

Not like this:

Social media is the new big thing → get into social media
→ develop social media strategy → wait, what?

"It's problematic that many businesses focus on existing and emerging technology and not on social behavior," says Paul Adams, Facebook's global brand experience manager. "Thinking about platform integration first, like Twitter or Facebook, or technologies first, like what could be enabled by 'mobile location' or 'real-time updates,' is the wrong place to start."

Adams says businesses need to realize that human behavior changes slowly, much slower than technology. So by focusing on behavior, a business is much more likely to create something that people value and use. He adds, "You're more likely to *protect yourself* from sudden changes in technology."

As you listen to people like Paul Adams and Olivier Blanchard and read the stories of successful social sellers, the opportunity is probably becoming clearer. *Designing* digital conversations in ways that produce what your business and its customers need is an exciting idea, and this idea of selling more by being selective about who to converse with, why, and how seems obvious. It makes perfect sense to converse in ways that generate customer inquiries—questions that you can help them solve. But where do you start with social media?

First, it's important to remember that smart marketers continue to invest in advertisements that garner attention and persuade customers. That doesn't cease. And you shouldn't run out and cut public relations or promotional budgets. That said, the businesses we've met—and will continue to meet—are selling off the hook largely because they're mixing in good, old-fashioned *direct response marketing*. They're putting behavior generation on the front burner; focusing on behavior is the best starting point.

"A lot of times people think that Web marketing is this whole new thing. But it's not," says author and former Distinguished IBM Engineer Mike Moran (www.mikemoran.com). "Web marketing is based on **response**. And people who understand response the best are direct marketers, the same people that are shoving catalogs and credit card offers in your mail box. They know what to do, and Web marketers need to follow them."

Brand is Behavior

What if the arrival of social media is an opportunity to align our behaviors with those of customers in a way that defines the brand itself? In other words, could social media marketing be our chance to *be the brand experience,* not merely build or enhance it?

The idea of using social media to prompt behavior is a logical one, but author, speaker, and leading branding consultant Jonathan Salem Baskin (www .jonathansalembaskin.com) encourages us to go further: to build and measure brands based entirely on behavior. Baskin is a former mass media ad-man who worked with Apple, Limited Brands, Blockbuster, and Nissan. But unlike most advertising executives, he's encouraging us to keep grounded in reality—that is, customer behavior. When designing any kind of marketing or advertising program, Baskin insists, "Always remember that consuming a message is *not* an action; taking an action is an action."

That's profound because while many of us believe a strong digital brand to be defined by the memorability of a trademark, Baskin and a handful of others say a new definition has arrived. Brand is behavior. No, it's not "a commonly held set of beliefs about what you deliver and how you deliver it," as some like to say. Neither is brand evidenced by its level of "social engagement." Brand is *created and evidenced by behavior,* period.

In other words, Baskin and other innovators say your brand *is* the tangible benefits actually delivered to customers: their total experience online and offline. As it turns out, this idea is a cornerstone of successful social selling. As we'll continue to learn, behavior is all that matters.

Baskin boldly proclaims, "Brand is behavior," in his seminal book, *Branding Only Works on Cattle.* He goes on to say that a digital brand is no longer what a company wants customers to feel or think. Business success is no longer a factor of how many times customers see, think, or hear about your brand name.

"Brand is no longer reserved to what your marketing department declares," says Baskin.

He says your digital brand is literally the real-time aggregation of everything you and your customers *do* together—how you behave, what you experience together, good and bad. It's qualitative and based on actual benefits your product or service produces. Brand and behavior are actually inseparable.

In this light, the social media opportunity becomes one of helping customers *experience* brand. Notice I said "helping." Social media is just one way to align a business's behaviors with purpose-driven actions of customers. If you think about it, social media isn't the only way a business can itself experience (or create an experience) alongside customers. If that's true, social media looks more like a cog in the overall wheel of your business. It's just one more "behavioral arrow in your quiver," and that's an important distinction when getting ready to design a "brand as social behavior" approach.

The Truth about Zappos

For instance, ask any marketing professional why Zappos is the raving success that it is. They'll probably mention social media within the first two breaths. Ask a Zappos employee, and they'll talk about culture and Twitter. But is that really true? CEO Tony Hsieh knows otherwise. Hsieh is one of the biggest social media success icons, but even he admits that social media is just one part of a larger "experiential engine." In fact, he often states that Zappos is a remarkably successful business because it qualitatively improves on the experience of shopping for shoes, *not* because of its use of social media or quirky culture. The total *experience* customers receive with Zappos *is* the Zappos brand, so let's keep perspective.

In the late 1990s, there were a handful of products that consumers would never, ever buy on the Web. Cars, sunglasses, and shoes were among them. But eBay, a variety of sunglass sellers, and companies like Zappos proved popular theory wrong. These brands delivered an astoundingly effortless, safe, and enjoyable *experience* to skeptical consumers. For them, brand is behavior. Today, these businesses are tapping into more sales by aligning experiences they create with customer need. Their behavior directly and consistently aligns with needs of customers.

Again, could Zappos be the successful business that it is because it understood that people wanted a better way to shop for shoes and then delivered one? Or does it prevail because employees Tweet and spread their joyful, quirky culture throughout the social media universe? The answer is obvious, especially when CEO Tony Hsieh admits, "The *telephone* is actually one of the best ways to build that human connection."

Hsieh, the quintessential social media businessman, says the telephone trumps social media. That's right, the phone is more effective in helping Zappos employees align their gestures in ways that constantly translate and cater to customer need and that create remarkable customer experience. Yet Zappos is often celebrated as the number one "social media–powered company." Go figure.

The truth is Twitter, Facebook, telephones, e-mail—none of these are the secret sauce. Even the telephone is just a tool. Zappos is giving customers what they've (rather secretly) been wanting: *a better way* to shop for shoes. As part of that process, the company aligns behavior of employees in ways that discover and cater to the evolving needs of customers. It creates unique, compelling experiences. Zappos uses a fantastic Web interface, the telephone, e-mail, and social media to be extraordinarily useful and convenient to customers. That's what Zappos calls "WOW."

Do the tools matter? You bet, and some are better than others. Sure, in some cases social media can get the job done better than the phone, but focusing on tools risks missing the opportunity. Likewise, focusing on the magical allure of the Zappos brand risks oversimplifying the company's success.

"Companies that successfully innovate always seem to find *latent* demand: needs that customers can't express and that competitors do not or cannot see," says Gunnar Branson of Branson Powers.

"Consider innovations such as the Internet, personal computers, digital media, and smartphones. Each one answered a powerful demand that few thought existed. Not many people could have said they needed those things *before* they were built, and yet once those concepts were introduced, the demand was fast, furious, and even overwhelming."

Indeed, Zappos did what most of us have a difficult time doing. The company went far beyond using new social media tools to build a unique corporate culture or brand. It innovated. As a result, the Zappos brand *is* behavior.

Much like QTCU, Zappos is *being* brand by aligning every move it makes with customers' behavior.

Focus on behavior

By now you might be wondering, "How can I pick the right strategy (and supportive technology) to help our business make social sell?" We'll address that more in chapter 4 when we put all of this to work. For now, Facebook's Paul Adams offers practical advice.

"Rather than try and predict which technologies will be dominant, I think the safer bet for businesses is to understand how these technologies will support human behavior and how they will help people do things they are struggling to do today," says Adams.

For instance, Adams says mobile technology looks like it could be a game changer because mobile handsets know who we communicate with the most, who we care about the most, where we are, where we've been, and probably where we're going! In the near future, handsets will know the things we buy. But that's leading to a lot of hype, speculation, and excitement. So Adams cautions business owners and managers to base their decisions on how a given technology will help people *do things* they are struggling to do *today*.

That's exactly what companies like HubSpot are doing: they're focusing on solving customers' problems. If you think Grader.com is cool, keep reading. We'll return to learn more about their expansive educational approach and the dividends it's paying. Because companies like HubSpot are *expecting* social media to serve clear, mature purposes—moving customers toward a trial (lead), sale, or upgrade, for instance. They're accomplishing business goals by helping customers do things they're wanting to do. And they're mixing in direct response calls to action with social media in ways that *create manageable behavior*.

> *"Rather than try and predict which technologies will be dominant, I think the safer bet for businesses is to understand how these technologies will support human behavior, how they'll help people do things they are struggling to do today."*

Disney Sells Off the Hook by Being Useful

Disney is another company that actively aligns its own behavior with customers' social needs. Like Burger King, Disney is using the concept of "being useful." For instance, it prereleased *Toy Story 3* theater tickets on Facebook by publishing its "Tickets Together" Facebook application (www.disneyticketstogether.com). In doing so, the entertainment giant improved the normally mundane process of buying movie tickets for groups of family or friends, similar to how Zappos improved the process of buying shoes.

Some entertainment companies make movie tickets available on Facebook in advance and at a discount just because they can, and they may sell a few tickets here or there. For most entertainment marketers, Facebook is seen as another place to push promotions. But Disney is choosing to make group ticket purchasing faster, easier, and more accessible. They're becoming useful to fans using social media, fans who are known to have a specific need based on how they shop: socially, in groups. The company is catering to a specific need by aligning its behavior with customers' known, preexisting behavior patterns.

Disney's Facebook application allows moviegoers to choose where and when they want to see the movie based on location. The application automatically displays local theater times. Checking out is as easy as adding friends to a list and submitting a charge card number. A Facebook event is automatically created so everyone is reminded of the date. Simple.

On the surface level, it may look like a gratuitous use of Facebook, simply using it as a virtual ticket booth. But the iconic entertainment company is actually producing new value for customers beyond its core product. Buyer and seller each experience improvements in their personal and business lives. Disney's team is using social media technology to sell in a new way, and they're doing it by *publishing* a tool that helps customers buy the way they want to: faster, easier, and in ways that earn occasional perks or discounts.

Much like Zappos did with shoes, Disney is improving the actual ticket-buying *process* for customers. The buying experience itself is improving, and that creates demand. Just as the founders of Zappos understood how people were buying shoes before Zappos was launched, Disney already knows the real-world (non-Web) social aspects of buying entertainment products. Customers are explicitly demonstrating needs all the time through their behavior.

In this case, friends typically go to the movies in groups. Disney realized this dynamic, and using Facebook, the company is leveraging how customers buy to prompt more ticket-buying activity. Disney knew Tickets Together would probably pay off before they even launched the application. The company looked inward for answers, to customers (not to external gurus or hip trends).

Think of it in terms of a problem and solution. Problem: organizing even a small group of friends to go see a movie together can be cumbersome. Solution: Disney makes group purchasing a snap. A discount element offers incentive to give it a try, and ideas like an automatic sweepstakes entry creates more excitement in the form of a game.

The Tickets Together application is becoming a powerful *utility*, and that's why customers love it. Given how ubiquitous Facebook has become to everyday life, Disney is integrating with the fabric of customers' daily existence. Sure, they're "bringing the ticket booth to the customer," if you will. But they're also making that ticket booth serve customers in new, useful ways, ways that match customers' preferred buying behaviors.

Remember, the secret sauce isn't Facebook or even the Tickets Together application itself. Once again, it's in the *design* of the tools: their functional purpose and ability to provide a highly useful experience within a realm that makes sense. Facebook, at its core, is entertainment, and so is Disney.

Disney is using our two key success principles. It's focusing on prompting customer *behavior* and making itself useful to Facebook-addicted customers. The company is catering to a behaviorally identifiable need and aligning its own behavior with customers by *publishing* an interactive tool—that is, a device that allows customers to do what they already want to do: buy tickets in groups without the hassle!

Intuit Walks the Walk, and Zooms Leads

Have you ever tried talking your way out of a situation you behaved yourself into? If you're lucky, it happened once when you were six years old and never again! Whether as a child or an adult, can you remember what it was like? Awkward to say the least. And you probably learned a lesson: talking your way out of situations you've behaved yourself into can be nearly impossible. It's best to "behave yourself out."

Think about it in a business context. Has your business ever tried to talk itself out of a negative situation it behaved itself into? If so, you now know what public relations is for! But was simply *telling* your customers enough? Consider Queensland Teachers Credit Union's experience earlier in this chapter and its solution. In the end, the business walked the walk and behaved its way out of trouble with its core market.

Although Intuit didn't get itself into a mess with customers, it did have a problem, and much like the Queensland Teachers Credit Union did, Intuit decided to behave its way out. The small business software company is always in need of introducing more business owners to its product line. To help identify social marketing opportunities, Intuit regularly identifies "pain points" of its target market. The company discovered prospects were having trouble getting started with social media. Many do-it-yourself–oriented business owners were reluctant to learn it. Others were scared of it or found it too technically daunting or time consuming. Yet they knew it was critical to their business.

So Intuit decided to *show* prospects how easy it was to do social media marketing. The company decided to actually help prospective customers solve a problem. In doing so, they designed a program that generates thousands of leads per month for its Payroll product. Of course, Intuit is no spring chicken when it comes to serving customers. They've been turning the idea of helping small- to mid-sized enterprises into billions in revenue for over two decades.

And although social media is new, Intuit had enough experience with ideas like digital communities to have learned a few things itself. Intuit was already making social gestures—offers that help small business owners. They got started in 2005 and knew firsthand that social media was all about service, but they also realized it's about selling.

The company came up with the idea of helping small business prospects actually grow, and they did it by offering something nearly all businesses need at some point: access to cash. They launched a grant program wherein businesses competed for needed cash. As part of the program, Intuit offered grant applicants a chance to get their feet wet with social media marketing.

By including this educational portion in its grant program, Intuit hoped customers would *prove to themselves* that social marketing was nothing to be scared of. The plan was to integrate the grant competition process with social media in ways where participants became comfortable with and good at using social media marketing. They might even have some fun doing it.

In 2010, the "Love a Local Business" campaign was born (www.lovealocal business.intuit.com). Intuit offers a monetary grant to a handful of lucky small businesses, the winners of a vote-based competition. To get the word out, the company started scrappy. Intuit used its own highly trafficked Web sites, but the team also tapped Twitter, Facebook, and other social networks to promote the competition. They also tested a bit of radio advertising.

Here's how Love a Local Business works. Upon arriving at the site, local business owners nominate their company to receive a grant. The process starts by prompting owners to apply for the contest. They're asked to provide name, business name, address, e-mail, and phone number. Participants are then asked to "share a few brief sentences about why you love serving your customers and community." This opens the door for passionate responses and more completed forms (leads). Overall, the application process is painless; it takes about two minutes.

Once the application is submitted to Intuit, the business owner is prompted to "get out the vote!" They can't win without votes. They're told, "Each vote is like a raffle ticket: the more votes you get, the more chances you have to become a monthly Finalist who wins a $25,000 Intuit Grant." In essence, participants are asked *to do something they already want to do*: become validated as a business owner and community member. Indeed, as a human being. Intuit is *tapping into the primal social instincts of the prospect.*

Intuit's design provides business owners with useful testimonials and tools to *immediately* earn votes in its Winner's Playbook. This toolkit is geared to increase chances of winning and give participants a useful Web marketing tool. You see, votes cast by friends, family, customers—anyone really—include a few brief words on *why they love the participant's business.* These supportive words are immediately displayable on the participant's Web site.

Testimonials

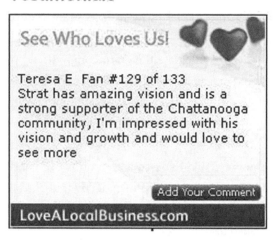

> See Who Loves Us!
>
> Teresa E Fan #129 of 133
> Strat has amazing vision and is a strong supporter of the Chattanooga community, I'm impressed with his vision and growth and would love to see more
>
> Add Your Comment
>
> **LoveALocalBusiness.com**

As part of "getting the vote" out, thousands of business owners become social media marketers, proving to themselves that they *can* do it.

Here's how the Winners Playbook works. Small business owners are immediately given the chance to use Facebook, Twitter, LinkedIn, Foursquare, customized banners, text messaging, and other Web marketing tools. Again, each tool is optional, but Intuit's integration with social networks is designed to help participants earn votes and testimonials from their fans. Owners thus begin a simple, multifaceted process that elicits votes for their business, increasing their chances of winning the grant.

Aside from providing cash to deserving businesses, Intuit's goal was simple: help thousands of prospective customers overcome fear of social media marketing by doing it successfully. Intuit realizes it cannot sell to a market without investing in it, and the company has been helping small businesses experience more success for many years now. Intuit knows that only good can come of this practice, but in exchange, Intuit's strategies *always* include generating leads for its product in exchange for the aid it provides.

The Winner's Playbook

Compete to win!
These tools make it easy to get more votes

Rally Support!
Tell your customers, friends and family that their votes can help you win. Start sharing »

Text2Vote
The newest way to get votes — now your customers and fans can text their votes for your business. Sign up for free »

Custom Banners
With up-to-date vote counts and nominations, they're a great addition to your website or blog. Get your banners »

Intuit Business Directory
Improve your online presence, track customer reviews, and more. See your business listing »

Improving on Early Success

Intuit's team realized that "Love a Local Business" was working and why it was working. But they felt it could perform better for the company. The group was convinced that far more applicants (leads) could be attracted with a slightly more compelling, relevant hook. Yes, many small businesses needed cash, perhaps more than in any time before in the company's history. Intuit's grant program was spot on, but the team asked itself a tough question as it tried to improve lead output.

Specifically, they asked, "*Why* do small businesses need cash? For what specific, urgent purpose?"

At that moment, given dire economic conditions, small businesses needed to hire. Local communities and the United States's national economy depended on jobs-based growth. More than anything else, the federal government, business owners, and Intuit needed businesses to start hiring again. *This* is what was *more relevant*: why businesses needed cash. Intuit's hunch was validated by an increasing amount of hiring-focused conversations within its social digital communities.

At the same time, the nation's largest payroll services and software provider was having a problem: too few businesses recognized Intuit's position as a leader in payroll, and current marketing programs weren't getting the message through. They weren't generating enough leads to grow the product.

Intuit's cross-functional team realized its fledgling Online Payroll product and Love a Local Business could be connected; they *should* be connected because doing so would give each the shot in the arm it needed because companies who are gearing up to hire are also likely to be interested in payroll products and services. The leads being generated would best serve the Online Payroll product.

The company decided to pour more budget into helping small businesses, increasing the quarterly grant total to $100,000. Love a Local Business now became a *hiring*-focused grant program for small businesses that needed to hire more employees. The voting, social media assistance, and the rest of the "moving parts" of the program were left intact. Participants continued to experience how easy social media marketing was, earned testimonials, and so on, all as a benefit of trying to earn votes.

Intuit's hunch was simple: attracting business owners who need money for hiring would be easier. Yes, they would also increase spending on Google AdWords ads to get the word out more widely. But this time would be different, mainly because a hiring-focused offer would be more *relevant to solving prospects' immediate problem*. And it was. Once making the shift, Web visitor traffic from paid ads and organic (non-paid, naturally occurring) search engine exposure saw a significant uptick. *Thousands* more small businesses signed up. *Being relevant* worked. Being focused on the market's "pain point" (hiring) earned Intuit more attention and more participants (leads).

Intuit was attracting and capturing information on a sizable, hiring-focused group of small businesses. Within ninety days of generating fresh leads, the payroll group began e-mailing prospects who had entered the hiring grant competition. Intuit began to delicately market the payroll product. And sure enough, prospects were responding: purchasing. As compared to Quickbooks customers (a sister product and brand), who were presented a similar payroll e-mail promotion, the Love a Local Business (hiring-focused) leads were converting to sale at a rate three times better. Even more impressive, Love a Local Business prospects who started purchasing Intuit's payroll software and services were *new* Intuit customers. Some had never even heard of Intuit before the campaign. Relevancy was working, earning attention and the sale.

Why It Works

Let's quickly review why Intuit's social media design works.

- Aligning behavior. The company is showing prospects how easy it is to be successful online marketers. It isn't using advertisements to *tell* customers. Intuit is taking action and asking customers to take action, too. They company is focusing on alignment of behavior, not messages.
- Relevance. Intuit is providing a contextually important answer to prospects' most urgent problems. The company gives cash to owners that need it most to solve an immediate problem.
- Looking to customers for answers. Intuit listens and understands that its target market already wants to be successful online marketers. They just need an incentive to get going. The company uses this knowledge to its advantage, using an *increasingly relevant* grant program as incentive.
- Interaction and direct response. The company is rolling out a traditional lead-generation promotion, not a flash-in-the-pan, attention-grabbing social media ad campaign. Intuit uses what it

knows will likely work. It creates mutually beneficial results for thousands of small businesses using a series of behavioral prompts.

- Innovation. Intuit asks itself challenging questions. The team instinctively wants to know what's holding customers back from buying its products. In this case, they realized customers' goals were being blocked based on fears, so they took action to eliminate uncertainty about getting started with what their product helps finish.
- Solving problems. In the eyes of participants, Intuit is a free, indispensable business coach helping customers overcome fears and *get things done* (market their business online and hire employees). Thousands of grant program participants who didn't win never felt like losers because they were suddenly marketing themselves online and using social tools to boot! In effect, Intuit's leads are overcoming a fear that is critical to their survival. They receive value from Intuit.
- Trust. Given how useful and relevant Intuit is, customers are more receptive to being pitched their goods and services.
- Facebook. Intuit is reaching beyond friends and fans to capture leads.

Consider also Southwest Airlines. Social media gurus tell us the airline's DING smartphone application (www.southwest.com/ding) "brings the ticket counter to the customer." True, but the mobile tool is more *useful* than it is portable or sexy. It connects with fliers' busy, on-the-go context and creates profitable behavior for Southwest. It gives customers a qualitatively better way to do what they need to do. For instance, fliers can check in as early as possible to get a better boarding designation. The airline is successful at filling plane seats for many reasons, one being how addictive it has made routine processes like getting a boarding pass.

Southwest's social media team is setting all the hype about the iPhone and mobile applications aside. They're asking themselves what's missing from the *experience* of booking tickets or checking in for a flight. The airline asks itself questions relevant to its customers' daily lives, rather than just following the pack. When they do, the right answers snap into focus: a better way to ticket and reschedule for the on-the-go, do-it-yourself customers that Southwest caters to.

The airline responds with a faster, easier, and more cost-effective airline booking and addictive check-in experience. And it's all portable. Many years ago it beat competitors at the online ticketing game, and today it continues to win the sales game using the same idea of *contextual usefulness*. Southwest's DING mobile and computer desktop application helps fliers how, when, and wherever they need it. It's a contextually relevant tool that meets the demands of no-nonsense travelers. It's not as funny, novel, portable, sexy, or memorable as it is relevant and useful.

Aligning Behavior, Solving Problems, *Being* Brand

Intuit, Zappos, SouthWest Airlines, the Queensland Teachers Credit Union, AnchorBank, and Logan Services—these companies are *being* brand by aligning their actions with customers' behavior. They're solving problems for customers and generating leads and sales in return. Similarly, Burger King knows that people want to eat hamburgers, fries, and milkshakes. But people also want a better Facebook experience, maybe even more than they want a burger! So the home of the Whopper helps customers improve their lives in meaningful ways.

Let's pause. By providing value that's in context with customers' lives, is Burger King "ethically bribing" customers into taking actions they (unknowingly) want to take anyway, one of those acts being to eat out more often? Let's face it: fast food companies are like most retailers these days. They're relying on being able to sell products at better prices or better margins, and that's becoming an increasingly difficult game to win. That's why *helping customers diagnose and solve problems* is an increasingly better strategy.

The businesses we're meeting are living proof: The answer to selling more with social tools is rooted in starting conversations that are worth having, conversing in ways that align the needs of buyer and seller, and *designing* conversations with customers in ways that generate inquiries and sales.

Reflection questions:

1. Be social but purposeful. Think about being social in terms of your business. Are you eliciting problems from customers so you can talk to them about the answers? Consider how this kind of idea plays a more powerful role than getting customers' attention. Think about the examples we discussed. Contrast them with your own social media campaigns, projects, or routine uses. How purpose-driven are your social media conversations? Are you talking with anyone who'll listen, or are you picking and choosing your conversations based on outcomes you're aiming to achieve?

2. Publish with a purpose. Are you already publishing to customers? For instance, do you engage in contract publishing or custom publishing? If so, how can you use existing assets and "fold them into" new, interactive (Web-based), direct response programs that net leads or sales?

3. Avoid monologues. Consider your current social media activities, everything you're doing to "join the conversation" like Tweeting, blogging, and posting updates on Facebook. Count how many activities involve talking with or talking at customers and those that are truly interactive. Consider calling a time-out on those that broadcast and do not interact. This will help you ensure your business isn't charging forward under the banner of conversation while actually practicing a monologue.

4. Score! Are your current social media practices causing you to miss the real opportunity to sell? Consider Twitter, Facebook, your blog, video—each of your social strategies. Score each based on its ability to interact with customers and prospects. Score this way: one point for broadcasting (low interactivity) and five for conversing (high interactivity). Do some interact more than others? Why? What about their nature is different than others? This will help you understand how focused your social media marketing is on getting attention versus identifying and capturing demand.

5. Stay in context. Communicating doesn't occur in a vacuum. Do you know how your blog or other Web content relates to the *context* in

which it's consumed by customers? Think of the conversations you're interested in having with customers and the context you're issuing the "conversation starters" within. How well do your conversation starters relate to the actual context of the customer? Are you confident that the assumed context is correct? How specific are your conversation starters, and are they leading consumers toward taking an action?

CHAPTER 3

TRANSLATE NEED (DON'T JUST LISTEN)

*"When you create a utility, you're creating
something that gives people time back.
It becomes less about information as pollution
and more about information to help
people get through life."*

Nick Law,
Chief Creative Officer, R/GA North America

WHAT will be your competitive edge? Selling products at lower prices and fatter profit margins? Helping customers diagnose and solve problems, becoming a successful "social seller?" Will you play the price game or design an approach that lets customers qualify themselves as candidates for products and services?

Businesses like Disney and Logan Services are selling off the hook by helping customers get more value from products and services they sell. Others like Intuit and Queensland Teachers Credit Union are helping prospects get important things done. Some are becoming experts in helping customers create more sales (Intuit), while others are focusing on rewarding customers emotionally (QTCU). In any case, these winners are making things happen for customers.

But to make remarkable things happen *consistently* for customers, we need a crystal-clear understanding of what matters to them. Being relevant 24/7 takes work. Sometimes customers' itches are obvious, so we just scratch 'em. But others are hidden, and let's face it, what customers need to accomplish in their lives changes like the wind. Now what?

That's why today's best social sellers are becoming *translators* of customers' evolving needs. They're using social media to make everyday office life easier. They're finding ways to discover and solve customers' problems by answering them quickly and easily. At the same time, they're making answers *super*-relevant to customers. For instance, Rachel Farris of PetRelocation.com publishes blog posts and video clips that always get discovered, read, shared, and acted upon. She does it quickly and easily. She earns more sales because the wisdom she shares is in sync with prospects' context, and she mixes in calls to action. She asks for the sale. Others are producing podcasts that always earn trial subscribers, product sample requests, or white paper leads. How do they do it? How do they *constantly* discover practical, doable ways to construct social programs that sell?

Many of the companies we've met are doing one thing exceptionally well: they're designing. But they're also translating, and that means they know *what and how* to design. They are continually:

1. **Prompting customers to signal** what they're most interested in, when, where, and why
2. **Publishing** useful, relevant tools and information that fit customers' context
3. **Planning processes** that guide empowered customers toward destinations they choose

In this chapter, we'll learn how people like Rachel Farris are making quick work of being *continually* useful to customers. You'll see how solving customers' problems actually makes your life easier because it produces a continuous flow of insights—*useful clues* for you to design social media programs around. Customers are giving us ideas all the time. Many times, picking up customers' signals simply means paying attention. Remember Marcus Sheridan from chapter 1? He started by writing down every question that was ever asked of him by customers. Simple. Yup, it's probably not as difficult to translate as you may think, so let's get started!

Now, if you've heard anything about "how to use social media," it's how important listening is. Pundits and gurus keep reminding us to listen to customers. It's as if nobody has been listening to them all along! But today's most successful, digital-savvy sellers reach further than listening. They're prompting customers to express themselves. Then, they're *responding* to those expressions of satisfaction, ire, confusion, or need in ways that sell off the hook. To illustrate the concept, let's start with one of the best examples I've found.

Drive Sales and Leads with Education

Business-to-business software company HubSpot serves online marketers of goods and services. You may remember this company from chapter 2's discussion of the Grader.com suite of Web site diagnosis tools. HubSpot's customers are everyday business people needing a better way to manage leads, and HubSpot sells software that can help do exactly that.

Inbound Marketing University (IMU) (www.inboundmarketing.com) is HubSpot's free marketing training and certification program. The company's educational service is rapidly "proving out" the translation concept I'm describing. For instance, imagine that a HubSpot prospect isn't ready to buy or take a free test drive of HubSpot's paid software solution. Let's also say the free Grader.com toolbox isn't doing the trick. The company offers IMU as another free option. Why? Because nearly every HubSpot prospect has burning questions about Web marketing, and IMU is a respected Web marketing resource, ready to answer. Of course, it's also serving as a lead generation program for HubSpot.

This should be a familiar concept to you by now—publishing relevant, useful tips and information that help customers solve everyday problems. But let's take a look at *why* HubSpot is choosing education and how it helps makes everyday office life so easy and fun for their staff. Educating prospects is an outstanding way to get them to signal what they're most interested in, when, where, and why. It's a very easy way for HubSpot to figure out how to design ways for customers to guide themselves toward Hubspot's products. Educating customers is a painless way for HubSpot's marketing team to figure out what matters most to customers. Oh, and by the way, HubSpot is teaching this exact same *translation* strategy to customers, helping everyone sell off the hook.

For instance, HubSpot customer Marcus Sheridan of River Pools and Spas credits the company with teaching him how to do *inbound marketing*, an increasingly popular term HubSpot coined. But Sheridan also says the company quickly started solving critical problems for him, and providing practical, new ideas that started growing his local fiberglass pool installation business—ideas like "blogging as a viable way to generate sales." To follow up on making that idea a reality in Sheridan's life, HubSpot empowers him with products that crank up the volume. Overall, they've convinced this skeptical business owner that Web marketing *can* be easier, more fun, and more profitable, and that controlling Web sites, making them generate more sales, *and* running a small business, all at the same time, *is* possible. How much so? Well, for starters, Sheridan is impressed at how an educational approach worked to net *him* as a customer!

Today, Sheridan practices inbound marketing, a term differentiating "old school" from newer Web marketing strategies—that is, the idea of a business getting found online by customers (and having customers call them, inbound), rather than trying to buy their attention through outbound telemarketing advertising.

You'll recall the old proverb, "Give a man a fish and you have fed him for today. Teach a man to fish and you have fed him for a lifetime." Well, that's what's powering much of HubSpot's word-of-mouth success in the Web marketing sphere. They're not just giving sellers software tools to help get the job done; they're selling *free* hope, coaching, and practical know-how. That's how they're hooking and landing remarkably loyal customers.

Layers of Benefits

The IMU teaches business people how to do what they need to do more than anything else: generate, nurture, and capture more business leads, more often. HubSpot's software solution helps with that. But then again, so does Microsoft Windows and its suite of Office products if you work hard enough. The difference is the layers of benefits an educational approach gives HubSpot and its target market; it puts HubSpot in a league of its own.

You see, IMU's students can be current or prospective HubSpot customers. When students complete courses and pass the Inbound Marketing Certification Exam (with a 75 percent or above score), they become Inbound Marketing Certified Professionals. HubSpots' graduates earn valuable credentials useful to their career path and creating more online sales. That's because they actually develop skills needed to execute better marketing programs, which is what the company's software is all about: making Web marketing produce more leads. In return for its gesture, HubSpot gets more qualified leads, more often.

HubSpot sells business lead-management tools to marketers. But unlike competitors, the company surrounds products with *services* that make customers more effective. HubSpot publishes free tools and services that customers don't just want or appreciate; they *really* need them. In fact, customers (perhaps like yours) are evolving to *expect* valuable, low- (or no-) cost tools from vendors.

IMU's online courses are taught by a faculty of leading marketing experts like pros like Chris Brogan (social media, www.chrisbrogan.com), Rand Fiskin (search engine optimization, www.seomoz.com), and Brian Carroll (lead nurturing, www.b2bleadblog.com), and suppliers like Eric Groves of e-mail company Constant Contact (www.constantcontact.com). In total, the program includes 16 one-hour classes, 10 reading assignments, and optional homework assignments for each class. In terms of pulling it off, the digitally delivered curriculum is highly scaleable. HubSpot records each class, lecture, or video once and then delivers each segment via the Web. Students learn virtually, on their computers. Classes are consumed by students at their own pace. Course curriculum is updated when needed.

In the end, students are getting better at blogging for business, search engine optimization, e-mail, social media, using advanced Web analytics, and so on. IMU's program teaches students and customers how to generate, nurture, and capture more business leads, more often, using techniques just like those HubSpot uses.

Let Customers Create Your Strategy

Here's where it gets interesting. IMU discovers and *translates* customers' evolving needs continually, over time, the company puts this knowledge to work, becoming more relevant. As a result, prospects qualify themselves as leads more often *and* dictate IMU's course curriculum. HubSpot's prospects literally coach the marketing team on what to do—how to design winning marketing campaigns—all by behaving naturally, like students.

As customers and prospects prepare for the Inbound Marketing Certification Exam, they interact with HubSpot. No surprise. But this behavior is providing useful insights to HubSpot like clues on current and changing needs of students, and that has benefits. For instance, it's helping HubSpot generate *and close* more leads by keeping course curriculum *relevant* to the most urgent, changing needs of prospects. It's helping them translate need: understand which fires students need to put out, when, where and why.

Can you think of a better way to listen to customers other than witnessing their behavior? Educating customers is a *reliable* way to *constantly* identify their changing needs over time or at any given moment. For instance, students may demonstrate intense interest in certain aspects of inbound marketing like social media or landing page optimization. Test scores, questions, and other information shared during the learning experience may signal either latent (early stage) or explicit (immediate) need. In fact, students often behave in ways that signal future or immediate need for a new HubSpot product. That's why the company studies them in whole (in groups) and individually. This identifies "need trends" that translate to new products and selling opportunities. That's another layer of value for HubSpot.

Think of it this way. The "behavioral byproduct" of educating customers is real-time, implicit insights on their needs. This information can be hard to come by. Even with the best market research practices, customers can be everything from confused to dishonest, but behavior tells all. Educating customers provides valuable insights—knowledge that you may otherwise never have access to.

For instance, Twitter may be what everyone needs to learn about today. But in a few months, social media may evolve in ways that deemphasize Twitter. If Twitter is becoming less important to customers due to the arrival of a new technology, the company sees it. Then, the team adjusts IMUs and Grader.com's relevance. Simple. HubSpot takes notice and starts offering free classes focusing on the newly emerging technology. In this way, customers and prospects become "marketing guides." HubSpot translates and redesigns.

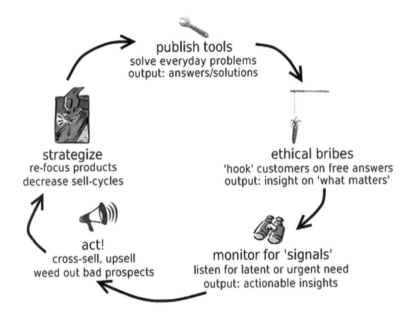

By noticing trends in what matters to customers, HubSpot is evolving its lead-generation program, Web marketing, *and* products faster. Even more exciting, the company is continually attracting more prospects and up-selling more customers, more often, all by improving the relevance of its educational offering. It's constantly adjusting curriculum to earn more of its customers' business. HubSpot stays relevant.

Businesses like HubSpot are proving that serving and selling *do* go hand-in-hand in ways that don't beat around the bush with customers. Being transparent with customers is not an issue because HubSpot's educational approach is designed to honor customers' dignity. When the company is selling, it's selling. When it's educating, it's educating. It makes promises and keeps them, and customers know exactly what's going on. HubSpot *is* selling with this educational technique. That's made clear throughout the process because doing so fosters deep trust.

Be in Context, Useful, Irreplaceable

Become a part of customers' daily lives.
Not an entertaining part, nor just an informative
part ... but a useful and irreplaceable part.
A part that's always in tune
with customers' changing context.

Companies like HubSpot and AnchorBank are constantly *translating* what users of their free tools need today and tomorrow. They simply don't miss a beat, and as a result, these businesses are having an easier time *creating meaning* for customers and profits for themselves because all of this translation is helping them find new ways to always be relevant, to remain *in context*. These companies have managed to become a part of customers' daily lives. Not an entertaining part, and not just an informative part, but a *useful* and sometimes *irreplaceable* part—a part that's always in tune with customers' evolving need. They're always in context.

But what does that mean in practical terms, and how can your business do the same? Let's look under the hood.

HubSpot doesn't miss a beat because of the process it's using to discover customers' evolving needs. The company is organizing its blogs, Facebook, LinkedIn presence, and so on in ways that *discover and act on* what matters most to customers. It's easy for them to understand what problems customers need solved because the business is always translating; it never stops.

For instance, Grader.com has evolved to a complete suite of free tools: Website Grader, Twitter Grader, Blog Grader, Facebook Grader, Press Release Grader, and others. HubSpot is also generating thousands of leads from blogging (www.blog.hubspot.com), niche blogging (www.manufacturing.hubspot.com), digital communities (www.inbound.org, LinkedIn, and Facebook), monthly tips-based Webinars, marketing kits (free videos and e-books), and focused resources it calls marketing hubs (www.hubspot.com/marketing-hubs).

For instance, River Pools and Spas' Marcus Sheridan ran into Grader.com when looking for free tools to help improve his e-commerce site. "I got an awful, awful grade on my Web site. I see myself as a competitive person. I got a seventeen-out-of-one-hundred, and immediately I was mad, but at the same time I thought, 'What can I do about this?'" says Sheridan, who willingly fell prey to HubSpot's approach.

"So I started researching HubSpot," he says. "Moreso inbound marketing, and there's been a few times in my life when stuff just made total sense. Inbound marketing was *clear* to me. It's what I knew was going on. I just didn't have a word for it in my head, and I started to diligently study it."

HubSpot is fashioning itself as *the* one-stop educational resource for all things inbound marketing. Today, the company is positioned to always be in context, no matter what. It literally owns the space it sells within ("inbound marketing") through continuing education. Pretty ambitious. Pretty smart.

HubSpot is publishing educational content and handy tools for marketers who need them—people who are struggling to improve online lead-generation skills using e-mail, affiliate programs, search marketing, and such. That's their itch, so HubSpot scratches it by publishing how-to tips in various formats, like downloadable video, podcasts, Webinars, and RSS feeds. HubSpot is constantly matching educational tools with practical needs of target prospects.

But let's be clear: HubSpot is a rapidly maturing, mid-stage technology business, and all of its activities may sound aggressive or maybe even scattered to you. So where we're headed next is not as advanced, but it *is* practical, focused, and aggressive. Let's take a closer look at how you can begin translating right away using what customers are already signaling to you. Plus, if you're already using blogs, Facebook, product and service reviews, and such, customers may already be communicating what they need. Let's start by learning how to take low-hanging insights and apply them to sell off the hook.

Turn Everyday Signals into Sales

When home goods purveyor Vintage Tub and Bath (www.vintagetub .com) noticed surprising customer feedback on its Web site chief operating officer Allan Dick sprung into action. The company's lean-and-mean marketing team quickly translated customers' hidden needs into more sales.

Vintage Tub publishes product reviews on its e-commerce site. But one day, Dick and his team noticed fanatical comments being published by a few customers—excited loyalists who were purchasing an under-performing product. The product was a toilet seat. But this was no ordinary toilet seat. This one was specially built for multi-age potty training and simultaneous adult use. It was a real Cadillac! Just flip the rim of your choice and have a seat!

Product review comments on the e-commece site seemed "over-the-top pleased." People were honestly excited to have found such a unique product. And that's when Allan Dick, who also claims chief plumbing evangelist status, took action. He asked himself the obvious question: if the product is so adored, why is it such a slow seller? No matter how much attention the product was given (on its Web site, in e-mail), it wasn't moving, but Dick wasn't ready to give up yet. He was convinced the product held potential. The comments confirmed his instinct was right.

Vintage Tub was listening. This small business was reading product reviews on its Web site, and based on customers' raves, the company spotted a hot seller waiting to happen. Sure, it was a very sanitary solution to potty training, and that's how it was being marketed—as a practical item. But Dick realized that the few customers buying it were doing so for *other* reasons. That's what they were "signaling" in their comments and purchase behavior.

The seat was aesthetically pleasing. "It looks great, not obvious unless you know it is there," published one reviewer. The seat was comfortable, sanitary, and convenient, and it offered progression for potty training, but that wasn't the problem that the seat was actually solving for customers who were buying it. One happy reviewer summarized the solution perfectly when she said, "Guest children and parents are impressed because it is one of those 'this is cool' items; it was purchased as a gift for my son's house, and based on the success, it is now officially *the gift* for new parents or grandparents from me. Great product!"

As it turns out, customers were more impressed with the seat's ability to surprise *gift recipients* in ways beyond function. The product was a very successful gift to give for a variety of occasions and family members. When customers were stumped on what to buy for a baby christening or a new mom-to-be, Vintage

Tub's ultra-cool potty seat was the answer. From new home owners to recent retirees (grandparents) and then some, customers were finding this product was a solution to their *gift-giving* problem. So Dick made the decision to position the seat as a novel (not just useful) home-warming, baby-christening, bridal, or baby shower gift. Vintage Tub joyfully repositioned how their toilet seat was being merchandised, pumping up the "life-stage gift" aspect.

In this example, customers signaled their problem: They needed a unique, novel, yet functional gift. The company responded with a new merchandising approach. As a result, Vintage Tub is selling more of their whiz-bang toilet seats, all because the business discovered *why* customers were actually buying the product and took action. The retailer is matching its merchandizing with customers' context, not following the advice of sheik gurus or hot trends. They quickly changed up the way an underperforming, high-margin product was being marketed and started selling off the hook.

If you think about it, most of us are happy knowing how many positive or negative reviews a product or service is getting, how many reviews are being produced or shared on average across all products, or how product reviews are helping turn more browsers into buyers. That's all well and good, but exceptional businesses like Vintage Tub and Bath aren't satisfied with marketing stats. They're constantly looking for ways to make social tools like product reviews *produce more sales*, open new markets, and increase customer loyalty.

> *Paying attention to customers' natural behavior is a simple yet often overlooked idea.*
> *Watch for their signals and put them to work. What you already know about customers is a great place to start.*

Businesses like Vintage Tub are always prompting customers to signal what they're most interested in, when, where, and why, using product reviews, for instance. Then, they're looking for clues, listening to customers, and learning about their shopping context. Finally, they're designing—or in this case, redesigning—processes to guide empowered customers toward destinations they choose.

By reading their own reviews, the company is continually discovering how buyers actually want to buy their products. Vintage Tub understands (translates) *why* customers actually need their goods and what problem they're solving with them. Dick and his team are using social media as tools to allow customers to *publish* reviews—to interact with other customers and the company itself—so it can reintroduce products in more relevant ways. They're bringing supply toward pent-up, hidden demand, and that's how the company sells off the hook.

At the highest level, Vintage Tub and Bath is *responding* to customers' problems with solutions based on insights gleaned from their behavior just like HubSpot is. In essence, Vintage Tubs is putting to use what it already understands about shoppers' needs. After all, all Dick and his team had to do was read product review pages; customers were already telling Vintage Tub what they needed.

You see, once we get going with social media, customers' natural behavior kicks in to help. One simply needs to pay attention to customers and know where to look for signals. Then you can begin putting the insights to work. In other words, the way customers shop for your product or service is already staring you right in the face. What you already know about them is a great place to start, and the good news just keeps on coming because once you start listening for these cues, life gets even easier, more opportunistic. That's what HubSpot and Vintage Tub are proving each day.

Apply What Customers Are Already Signaling You

Whole Foods Market's mobile smartphone application is focused on matching customers' shopping context. For instance, the Whole Foods' app makes meal suggestions based on shoppers' specific health conditions. It even suggests items to help in-store shoppers whip up a meal based on foods already stocked in their pantry. The natural foods supermarket focuses its widely adopted mobile app on satisfying customers' needs at that very moment to create demand for its products. People buy more because they're being prompted by a tool that caters to their context.

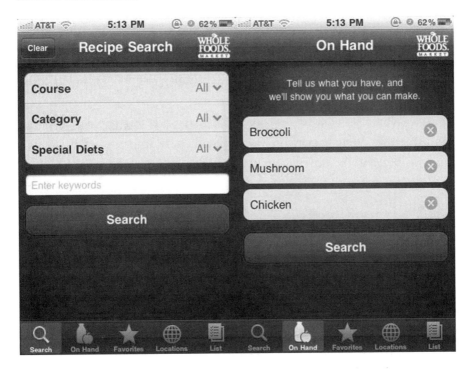

Worth noting, the grocery store's mobile app provides recipes, but it doesn't stop there. It helps customers customize meals based on a number of unique scenarios all relevant to the specific, individual context of each shopper—practical needs like budget, health, and frugality. Because the company *already understands* the basic shopping contexts of customers, designing the functionality of its tool is a snap.

Let's hit pause for a moment. Is Whole Foods merely making its products available on devices like iPhones in "easy-to-shop" ways? Or is the grocery chain qualitatively improving the experience of shopping its stores? If you think about it, this company is inducing on-the-spot sales by providing solutions to shoppers' problems within specific yet flexible contexts.

Does Whole Foods already know how its shoppers shop? Certainly. It knows, for instance, that eating in ways that improves health and wellness is an issue for customers and how increasing food costs are relevant concerns in a slowing economy. Much like your customers, they're far more price-driven now than ten years ago. You see, Whole Foods is selling off the hook by being more useful to customers in compelling but familiar ways, and they're not just bringing the store to the customer using a sexy mobile tool. Is it fun to use? Sure! But they're giving customers a *practical* tool, one that helps meal-planners navigate themselves toward destinations *they* (customers) choose: Whole Foods's products.

What could be next for the grocer? Perhaps allowing people to actively *express* their shopping scenario in ways that don't intrude on privacy. Customers could begin using the mobile app to actively signal how they are shopping in ways that serve both buyer and seller. Think shopper-savings card on mobile steroids.

Be Innovative:
Exploit Customers' Dislikes

Increasingly, creating a landslide of sales requires us to exploit customer dislikes. Now, I know that sounds crazy. In a world where "liking" has taken center stage, it seems illogical to suggest what customers like is *not* a key component to selling off the hook. But it may not be because what customers do *not* need matters more than ever. In fact, prompting customers to signal what they're *not* interested in is often what makes the difference.

Of course, it's a good thing when customers express positive sentiment, but the act of being "liked" on Facebook doesn't (alone) cause sales. Neither does it compel large numbers of customers to buy. That's because knowing what customers like or need does not help us discover *unmet* need. In other words, we're not able to take advantage of significant, sometimes explosive demand that exists but has yet to be realized.

What I'm getting at is this: how can your business become the next Zappos? The short answer is to get swept away by preexisting, unmet demand.

Gunnar Branson, CEO of Branson Powers (www.bransonpowers.com), is helping businesses do just that: create more sales with social marketing by tapping into what customers *do not* like. And sometimes the payoffs are huge. Why? Because people tend to be more specific about true needs when they're being critical. For instance, Branson points out how demand for light existed long before electric light bulbs. Heh, lots of demand there! And demand for instant information and communication certainly predates the Internet. Again, lots of people wanted that, too. Unmet demand is often very difficult to pin down, define, and understand. "Because," says Branson, "customers have a difficult time expressing what they need when what they need has yet to be known to them. But they know what they want when they see it!"

"Asking customers 'What do you want?' usually produces the answer 'more of what I have right now, but for less money,'" says Branson.

More and more, companies are investing in adding more features to products and services but only to end up discounting the price. Why? Branson believes this happens because most businesses end up following what market research tells them to do. They're investing in answers to the wrong questions.

"Companies that successfully innovate always seem to find latent demand— demand that customers cannot express and that competitors do not—or cannot—see," says Branson.

Again, think Zappos, or Apple with iPods, iPads, and iPhones.

Why didn't customers express need for a better way to buy shoes or a lighter, simpler way to enjoy higher quality music on the go? Because they couldn't fathom it, not because they didn't want or need one! Branson points out that a nineteenth-century focus group on personal transportation would probably have shown demand for better horses, less expensive maintenance, more comfortable carriages, or longer lasting riding boots. It's unlikely that anyone would have asked for a car (a horseless carriage). Automobiles had yet to be imagined by those who needed them. Of course, once Ford scaled production of automobiles, demand exploded to the point that everyone had to have at least one! Similarly, it only took 8 years for Apple to sell 250 million iPods.

The questions we ask ourselves and our customers are actually the key to unlocking explosive, unmet demand. Legendary media theorist Marshall McLuhan used to put it this way: "Sensible people deal with problems, and that's why 90 percent of events that are problems get all the attention." Great thinkers like McLuhan, Branson, and others say we should be focusing on the other 10 percent. That's where the opportunities are to create bigger, more valuable solutions. Of course, if McLuhan is right, the opportunities in any situation are the things most of us are not looking at.

For example, CEO of Hinton and Company (www.hintonandco.com) Michael Hinton says, "Consider the problem of garbage in the streets, which seems to be a problem in large cities. If we pay attention to the problem, our eyes are drawn to the actions of people who don't appear to care and throw stuff on the sidewalk. Perhaps we should pay attention instead to the opportunities, the people who care."

In other words, it's difficult to get in the habit of seeing opportunity among the minority of people who don't throw trash on the street. It's hard to envision that small percentage of eco-conscious folks supporting recycling programs before such programs existed. Yet in the early days of urban recycling, that's where the unseen, unmet demand was.

"What can you do to shake yourself out of the approaches and routines of sensible people? Ask yourself what isn't a problem in your life," says Hinton. "If McLuhan is right, that's where you need to look to find your opportunities."

But remember: nobody even knew they needed an iPod, a recycling program, or an automobile before they were built. As it turns out, our customers have a difficult time expressing what they need when what they need has yet to be known to them. But they know what they want when they see it, and that's when we can sell off the hook.

Fix Dislikes and Drive Incremental Sales

European grocery store Tesco (www.tesco.com) put this idea to work. Like Whole Foods, the supermarket started applying what they *already knew* about customers. But unlike Whole Foods, Tesco zeroed in on a specific customer *dislike* to drive incremental sales—transactions it probably wouldn't normally have a shot at. Sure, Tesco is listening to customers' chatter about their brand in social spaces. But the company is also taking advantage of what customers are *already known to dislike* outside of online social spaces.

Much like you may understand how a segment of customers shop, Tesco knows how people shop for wine. The company has been selling wine long enough to know. For instance, in many tasting scenarios, wine enthusiasts are impulsive, and it can be frustrating to want something yet be forced to spend a lot of energy hunting it down. Even if you don't drink wine, I'm sure you've been there: "There must be an easier way than this!"

As an example, imagine relaxing at a friend's party. He or she pours a glass of remarkably enjoyable Merlot that is completely new to you, or maybe you're a Chardonnay fan. You could be at a party or a restaurant with a colleague enjoying the same experience. This wine is so remarkable that you simply *must* know where it can be accessed and at what price. Heck, if you could, you'd have a case delivered to your place! In the past, you would need to scramble for pen and paper, write down the name, vintner, and year of the wine, then trek back home to the Web or visit a store. But in these kinds of scenarios, wine aficionados often want to order it right on the spot.

The dislike (problem) is obvious: The process of buying a newly discovered wine on a whim isn't very easy. The context of this situation doesn't match well with the labor-intensive process of buying wine, and people just don't like when that happens.

So Tesco decided to key on this dislike, to give excitable wine enthusiasts a way to research and purchase newly discovered thrills simply and quickly, all by snapping a picture of the bottle's label using a mobile device. Providing a mobile application makes perfect sense based on what Tesco understands about its customers' behavior—that is, the *context* in which wine lovers make purchase decisions. Tesco understands that how, when, and where wine lovers discover an exciting, new wine offers potential to sell it. Considering the disconnect between the customers' desire and the shopping process, Tesco saw untapped opportunity.

So Tesco provides a mobile application (www.oth.me/wineap) allowing customers to access full details about the wine instantly and within their immediate context, anywhere, any time. Information like price, availability, and an option to order a case are accessed by snapping a photo of the label. The software application uses visual cues to locate the wine in its database and displays relevant information.

Let's hit pause and catch our breath for a moment. Is Tesco creating a sexy application during a boom in mobile smartphone popularity? In other words, is Tesco following the trend of bringing the store to the customer by offering a "me, too" mobile app? Or is the European grocery giant taking an *existing* understanding of how customers discover wine and putting it to work? Are they focusing on a broken process (a customer dislike) and offering customers a shortcut?

By offering this mobile tool, Tesco is making a gesture (an act) that helps customers discover and sometimes buy in a more enjoyable, practical way. Why? Because the company *already knows* what customers need based on behavior they display and based on what they *do not* like about the "traditional wine discovery and buying" process. Sure, that's pretty cool. But even more exciting, Tesco's super-contextually–relevant response sets the grocer up for a return gesture—a purchase. Even cooler.

Let's consider one more question: is Tesco using mobile technology to help shoppers buy wine by "leveraging mobility?" What does that buzzword actually mean anyway? Or is the company improving the process of getting product knowledge into the hands of a niche customer group when and where they need it? Are they speeding up access to vital, needed information about wine that has a chance to spur a purchase?

Tesco's customers have always wanted to purchase wine in "offline" social contexts, but they didn't have a way to do it. Yet with everyone carrying a smartphone, mobility becomes a helper. But it doesn't happen "just because" it's possible, as pundits and gurus claim. It happens because of *how* a large group of people have always been wanting to buy wine, what they've always *disliked* about how it works today. Again, sometimes you don't need to be listening, just paying attention. In Tesco's case, they're using what's *already known* about customer dislike and creating tools that prompt the desired behavior—in this case, a sales transaction.

It's Always Season

As it turns out, many businesses are expert translators; they just don't realize it yet. For instance, let's take the technology piece of what I'm describing out of the picture because the truth is you don't need to be publishing on the Web to open new markets, boost profit margins, or extend selling seasons. All you need to do is have a business that pays attention, analyzes, and reacts.

Factory Card and Party Outlet (now a part of www.partycity.com) is living proof. Upon opening its very first e-commerce Web site, the party goods retailer noticed a strong demand for adult and children costumes—those that historically only sold in-store during one season, Halloween. Once the e-commerce store was up and running, remnant Halloween costumes were selling fast— *really* fast—clearing out excess inventory well before January 1. What was going on here?

The company learned that customers were snatching up costumes as corporate gag gifts, *not* for next year's Halloween season. Adult costumes were in demand for a variety of year-round occasions that called for pranks and various shenanigans. Many Halloween costumes for young girls were also popular year-round as part of increasingly popular dress-up games and parties.

Normally, the stores-based company had to store excess Halloween costumes and clear them out the following year or sell them at cutthroat prices in the wholesale aftermarket. But by monitoring demand and inventory levels for products and interacting directly with customers on the Web, the retailer learned how customers were actually using the products. They were solving an entirely new problem that the company never knew existed!

Factory Card and Party Outlet translated this insight into bigger profits and year-round buying seasons for select products. The company now makes all excess costumes, party favors, gifts, tableware, novelties, and so on available year-round on its e-commerce site, sometimes at full price. By listening (monitoring inventory levels), analyzing, and acting, the company was able to sell off the hook.

Might your company be too? Take the "social techie" piece out. Are you occasionally finding ways to open new markets, boost profit margins, or extend selling seasons? How can a behavioral approach to social media help supercharge your results?

Spur Repurchase, Referrals, and Advocacy

Okay. Can we take the idea of translation and apply it to reshape products in ways that encourage customers to buy them more often or to redesign services, injecting them with more value to drive repeat sales or upgrades? How about carving out profits through supply chain efficiencies or merchandising improvements? Social marketers inside today's most dynamic companies are doing all of these things, but the idea itself is not new. Ideas like product development and business process reengineering are actually quite old. They're merely being made easier by the Web.

For instance, companies like Vintage Tub and Bath and Factory Card and Party Outlet are creating "discovery feedback loops." These power more sales by improving ability to discover insights on customers' needs and changing contexts. What customers read, say, share, complain about, watch, listen to, rate, and consume are fair game in understanding their changing needs and behavior more deeply. It's exciting to be discovering changing customer context in real time, but it's what's being done with this context that counts; that's what's making social media sell.

For instance, online reviews are practical, accessible "discovery posts" for manufacturers like Newell Rubbermaid, owners of baby products brand Graco. But the company isn't just publishing reviews to convert more browsers to buyers on Web sites. Graco (www.gracobaby.com) is driving incremental and repeat direct-to-consumer sales by improving product design and customers' experiences.

For instance, Graco's social marketing team was wisely monitoring product review feedback across Gracobaby.com and retailer sites. Staffers discovered a large number of negative product reviews for Graco's Produce Saver food storage product. The company contacted disappointed customers to understand why. It learned the problem wasn't a faulty product. Instead, customers were having difficulty setting up the product for proper use. They were complaining about the product's inability to keep fresh produce fresh, but they were not following instructions properly. Customers were inadvertently blaming the product for a bad experience.

Graco quickly alerted its product design and packaging team to make instructions more plainly visible. As a result, positive reviews *and* sales increased significantly. More importantly, customers changed their behavior. The product was actually an excellent one when used properly.

Before social media, the company was not able to *quickly* and directly (with consumers) identify problems. Retail stores would have sent products back, and Newell Rubbermaid might have chalked it up to an unpopular product, but the social Web provided a faster path to qualify the problem and relieve it. In a way that boosted sales because the company was able to quickly translate customers' *real* (unseen) problem. It then responded in a way that gave customers the fix they needed so badly.

So the idea of translation (and its components) can be applied to re-shape existing products and services in ways that encourage customers to buy them more often. This involves injecting them with more value to drive repeat sales or upgrades. But this idea is not exclusive to the Social Web or interactive media. It's merely supercharged by these advances.

Follow Customers, Not Trends

Tesco, Factory Card and Party Outlet, Whole Foods Market, Graco ... all of these businesses are, in essence, following customers, not trends. They're letting customers provide the when, where, why, and how that powers their translation strategies. Customers are signaling what's relevant and most needed. The businesses respond accordingly.

When J and O Fabrics (www.jandofabrics.com) needs inspiration or guidance on where to take its social media game plan, it just says, "HEY." Literally. HEY started on a whim, but it's now a practical part of the fifty-year-old, family-run business's strategy. Using Facebook, the company regularly shouts out to the arts-and-craft–focused folks it serves, asking them what's important. This gives the company a chance to let customers carry some of the brainstorming weight and contribute ideas for blog story topics. For instance, "HEY—What's the first thing you ever made on a sewing machine?" or "HEY—What sparks your creativity?" For this retailer, it makes practical sense to prompt overly willing customers and prospects to provide ideas. Crafting customers just love to join in; they're very vocal online.

J and O Fabrics
Word to the Wise: Remember "iron-on" requires heat and pressure only. No steam.

2 hours ago · Like · Comment

15 people like this.

 I find that some iron-ons shrink slightly (without steam) and can cause bubbling on some fabrics. I tend to pre-shrink by very lightly and quickly ironing over the interfacing on a scrap of fabric and immediately pulling it off then pressing onto the piece to be sewn. I know you can pre-shrink by rinsing in hot water but my way save time.
2 hours ago · Like · 2 people

 That's good to know. I actually wasn't aware of that. Thanks for the hot tip;)
2 hours ago · Like

 Also get one of those teflon pressing sheet so your iron won't get full of any gunk from over flowing adhesive, or flipped ends, etc.
2 hours ago · Like

 Yeah, I didn't know that, either!
2 hours ago · Like

Write a comment...

Similarly, "Fab Fab of the Day" and "Sewing Tip of the Day" are two very successful Facebook campaigns that J and O Fabrics is investing time in because tips and tricks are what customers have always been interested in. It's what they actively gobble up. Customers want, value, and share the company's knowledge with others. "Fab Fab of the Day" and "Sewing Tip of the Day" focus on useful tidbits on hard-to-find or novelty fabrics and practical sewing tips. By providing a regular stream of tips-and-tricks, the company is increasing Facebook fan count. But more importantly, they're making more Facebook-generated sales more often, in part because what the business is publishing, providing, or promoting (doing) is *more relevant* to everyday needs of customers.

Here's how it works. The company regularly publishes tips on Facebook.

This is generating ideas among customers and more tips from customers themselves. Sometimes the company's initial bit of advice relates to solving larger problems, and community members jump in to point that out. Of course, all this activity gleans more attention to the *solution being provided* (not J and O Fabrics) across the social networks of those commenting and sharing more tips. Thanks to promotional activities (discussed in more detail later in the book) and clear, balanced calls to action, the strategy is occasionally spurring purchases.

> *Consider the customer behaviors or preferences you already know about to discover what works. Answers to questions like "what should we be doing on our blog?" become more obvious. What you should be investing time in suddenly leaps out.*

J and O is proof positive: When we consider known customer behavior patterns (or preferences), we can discover what works. Answers to questions like "what should we do now on our blog?" become more obvious. What you should be investing in suddenly leaps out.

J and O Fabrics is constantly prompting customers to help in plotting a winning social media course. The business notices what customers are *already doing*, or are willing to do, in social spaces, like crafters' propensity to share tips and upload photos of creations. The retailer then makes practical decisions about turning those behaviors to its advantage, often by mixing in traditional promotions. We'll look more deeply into how J and O creates so much selling activity with Facebook and blogs in chapter 6.

Consider USAA bank (www.usaa.com). When this financial institution asked itself "what should we do next with digital technology?" it considered what it *already knew* about its customers environment. Like J and O Fabrics, this bank's online business decisions are driven by customer behavior, not by the experts or trends.

For instance, many banks allow account balance, transfers, and payments to be made via the Web, but USAA was among the first to go further. The bank created a service allowing anyone with a desktop scanner to instantly and safely deposit a check from home. Its pioneering Deposit@Home was widely adopted by customers. Just slap the check down on your scanner, press go, and within a few moments, it was confirmed, securely deposited. It was a hit based on its usefulness. Being useful was "what was working."

Not stopping there, USAA was first to offer customers a way to deposit checks simply by snapping a photo. Today, the bank's @Mobile smartphone application serves a clear, simple purpose for customers on the go. It's deadly useful. Depositing a check isn't sexy, but it's what people do every day. It's what people *need*. More importantly, it's what customers *already demonstrated* they valued based on the success of Deposit@Home. That customer behavior was a key decision-making point for USAA. Customers were signaling they found strong value in the Deposit@Home tool.

Today, mobile technology serves the vital needs of USAA's customers, and the bank knew it would. Yes, its customers have a love affair with mobile. Most of us do. We're addicted. But USAA's decision to invest in @Mobile was based on what customers were *already doing*. Its customers were already using a similar desktop scanner check deposit tool. USAA set its course based on observable customer behavior. It didn't chase a hot trend. When creating its strategy, the bank asked itself, "What's been working lately with customers?" rather than "Should we create a mobile application?"

Customers were already telling USAA how they needed to deposit checks. They were using Deposit@Home. USAA just needed to notice. The bank didn't copycat or mimic a leading financial institution. Neither did it follow the trend to create mobile applications for iPods and Blackberry smartphones. It let its customers' behavior set the course.

More and more, social savvy companies are evolving by trusting their own instincts and turning to customers for cues on how to proceed, and they're not hesitating to use what they already know works to exceed customer expectation.

A Common Approach

All of the innovative companies we've met are forever committed to doing one thing very well: translating. That is, they are continually:

1. **Prompting customers to signal** what they're most interested in, when, where, and why
2. **Publishing** useful, relevant tools and information that fit customers' context
3. **Planning processes** to guide empowered customers toward destinations they choose

The most successful social media marketing programs work because they're designed to, and they're as useful to marketers as they are customers because everything these programs do prompts an expression of need so marketers can *hear, analyze, and respond.*

For instance, Vintage Tub and Bath gives customers the chance to express themselves through Web-based product reviews. But then the company reads them, looking for clues that reveal *how* customers are shopping for or using their products, all as part of a larger effort to increase sales. Who would have thought that a toilet seat would make such a hot-selling gift item? Certainly not Vintage Tub's management team. This is just one company that's making a habit of listening to customers and then applying "learnings" in ways that match customers' shopping context.

Newcomer Hubspot realizes that being *the* hands-down educational resource for its market is far more effective than trying to gain attention using advertisements. In fact, they're proving that marketing in such an innovative way can produce dividends. Their IMU curriculum is even being made available to college professors who want to help cement the concept of inbound marketing. The company is reaching into the classroom of secondary education institutions and looking for leads! Is HubSpot translating or boldly defining? Perhaps a little bit of both.

Okay. We've taken a deeper look at how leading businesses are inventing and executing practical processes—social media programs that reach beyond attention—and how they're winning more customers, more often by finding and translating need using social media. But before we start applying what works within your business, let's take a moment to come up for air. Let's have some fun and give critical thought to "all things social."

Reflection Questions:

1. Show and tell. How can you start swapping information with customers—your helpful knowledge in exchange for insight on their need? Answering this question will help you discover ways to start *showing* customers you've got answers to important questions.

2. Hide and seek. Most businesses are already creating value for customers beyond lowest price. Where are you adding value to customer relationships off the Web? For instance, what practices are you investing in that coach (at no cost to) customers? How can social media supercharge that? Is there an opportunity to build on what you're already doing for customers in ways that add value to the experience (i.e., by publishing information on a blog or a mobile application)?

3. Behave! What are customers already doing in social spaces that gives you signals on what's important to them today? Also, if customers are publishing product and service reviews, would they be likely to take other actions if they perceived a direct benefit? What could those actions and benefits be, practically speaking? Should they be based on your goals? Now consider the next steps to make your idea real.

4. Find a role model. Is there a good translation process already occurring within your business? Look around. Identify a component (person?) of your organization that translates well. Consider fan mail, hate mail, Better Business Bureau complaints, in-store conversations with customers, product reviews, telemarketing trends, and so on. What are you doing in the physical world that listens and gives clues on what matters to customers? Are there opportunities to close the loop, to take those insights and act? For instance, publish responses to those insights that move customers toward evaluation, selection, or recommendation of your product or service.

5. Target dislikes. Be practical. Use automated Google Alerts (www .google.com/alerts) to scout for and retrieve negative feedback on products or services you sell. Peer across the Web for very specific phrases that are typically used to issue complaints or dissatisfaction.

Use practical social media tools like Twitter search to gather up intelligence on dislikes in ways that don't consume precious time. For instance, could you invite complainers to vent frustrations in more detail on a blog you own or e-mail you more details at an e-mail address you provide? What follow up actions might you or your team take on the insights these dislikes povide?

CHAPTER 4

THIS IS EVOLUTION, NOT REVOLUTION (OR, WHY YOUR SOCIAL MARKETING DOESN'T SELL)

"In times of universal deceit,
telling the truth becomes
a revolutionary act."

George Orwell

BIGELOW Tea (www.bigelowtea.com) was excited to apply social media in ways that created sales. The company's advertising agency suggested the international tea giant start conversing more with customers. According to "the experts," sales always materialize by entering the conversation. This is Social Media Revolution 101. Or is it?

Bigelow hatched a YouTube video campaign. Bigelow's CEO began broadcasting on-the-street interviews with tea drinkers and sports legends who drink Bigelow's tea (www.youtube.com/user/bigelowtea). Soon afterward, the company's ad agency boasted in trade journals that the videos caused sales to increase. Now this got my attention, so I inquired as to how the agency did it—how the videos were inducing more tea consumption. I wanted to feature Bigelow's success story in this book.

But rather than learning more about how the campaign worked, I was repeatedly told that the result was true. No matter how many times I asked *how* the YouTube videos caused buying behavior among consumers, I got the same reply: sales went up.

"But that wasn't the question!" I kept thinking to myself. I was getting peeved.

Remember that old public service, anti-drug advertisement with the photo of an egg frying in a pan? "This is your brain on drugs," it read. I couldn't help but ask, "Could this be your ad agency on social media gurus?" Or maybe you prefer the Wizard of Oz: "Pay no attention to the man behind the curtain!"

Now a rational person might ask if Bigelow's ad agency is crazy? Irresponsible? Or am I the one who's crazy, stupid, or just plain wrong for asking questions? I concluded it was none of the above. That's when it hit me. There's a fox in the hen house. Investing in something and without good reason claiming it's paying back dividends isn't smart. What is going on here?

The Revolution Will Be Scrutinized

I started thinking. We business folk are putting a lot of stock in this "social media revolution." Do we risk caring more about traffic to our Web sites than business leads? One day, might we start measuring success in terms of friends and fans on Facebook rather than sales? Aren't we already today?

"Return on investment is still a question mark for most social media 'experts' in spite of the fact that (a) it has remained the same since the dawn of commerce, (b) every first-year business major can tell you what it is, and (c) most social media consultants cost a lot more per day than their expertise in basic business concepts seems to warrant," says Olivier Blanchard of BrandBuilder Marketing.

Could the social media revolution be putting relatively trivial pursuits in front of what *really* matters, and might our trusted social media guides actually be selling obstacles, rather than helping us achieve the real goal?

Think about how you are using social media today as part of your business.

For instance, let's say you're already using Facebook, Twitter, or blogging. You're probably updating, posting, tweeting, or "engaging" customers. But could engaging just be advertising with a fancy-pants name? Think about it this way: Does your day-to-day life involve *using* social media tools or *designing* interactions with customers in ways that sell?

Might you be reacting, rather than planning—"just doing" social media? And if so, could this be preventing you from selling more online? Did it prevent Bigelow?

Have We Lost Track of the Goal?

Outside consultants and digital gurus often try to get business-minded folks hooked on short-sighted ideas: beliefs they (gurus) have a financial stake in but that don't connect to outcomes like sales. One example is the notion that occupying time with a customer (engaging them) will cause them to buy. Another is "the rules governing business have radically changed." This is the fundamental idea behind the social media revolution itself. Of course, there's the idea that we've lost control of the conversation with customers. Never mind that we never really had control. And don't forget "social currency." Have you ever wondered which CEOs are satisfied with earning social currency rather than dollars or euros? We hear so much about these CEOs in books and keynote speeches given by social media gurus. But where are these people? Of course, these chief executives exist only in the minds of their inventors.

> *Could the result of unbridled enthusiasm for social media be combining with our urgent need to create results but in ways that don't serve us well?*

All of this nonsense raises a serious question. Could the result of unbridled enthusiasm for social media be combining with our urgent need to create results but in ways that don't serve us well? It seems all the excitement is causing many of us to continue down a familiar path: *Broadcasting messages* at customers rather than *designing interactions* with them: meaningful *exchanges,* "give-and-takes" that connect with sales.

Given the rush of nearly every living soul into the social Web and all the revolutionary fanfare, could we be losing track of what we set out to achieve?

Making Twitter Sell

But there are success stories, and there *is* a practical formula to achieve sales. For instance, enterprise communications provider Avaya (www.avaya.com) is manufacturer of the popular Audix voicemail system. This multi-billion dollar company needs a constant stream of inbound business leads for its hardware, software, and services products. Twitter fits the bill. In fact, Avaya is closing six-figure contracts using the microblogging service, and they can prove it was social media that netted the lead.

This is one big company that hasn't lost track of the goal. Avaya is wisely using Twitter's search function to monitor for signals emanating from their own (or competitors') customers. Across the vast, babbling Twittersphere, the company's social media marketing team is listening in for specific kinds of opportunistic signals. When they hear one, they spring into action.

The company literally listens for cues from prospects expressing purchase intent or frustration with problems. According to Paul Dunay, Avaya's former global managing director of services and social marketing, the team monitors for key phrases used by Tweeters and acts accordingly. For instance, a staffer may find a prospect expressing a specific need or who is intent to switch service providers. This allows Avaya to step in and assist the prospect.

That's what happened in June 2009. Avayas team discovered a fifty-seven–character tweet. This started the relationship with a potential customer:

> "[…] or avaya? Time for a new phone system
> very soon," the prospect's tweet read.

Moments after the tweet was posted, an Avaya team member spotted it and responded by tweet:

"@[customer]—let me know if we can help you—we have some Strategic Consultants that can help you assess your needs."

The potential customer did just that. And 13 days later, Avaya closed a $250,000 contract.

For Avaya, Twitter isn't seen as another channel to grab at attention by broadcasting discount promotion codes to anyone who'll listen. Sure, it uses the microblogging service to get the attention of prospects with outbound messages, and it listens for and helps disgruntled customers who are having problems. But it doesn't stop there. Avaya uses social tools to discover demand in various stages, and then chases it. In this instance, the customer's need was immediate. In other cases, customers need to be nurtured along over a longer period of time. So that's what Avaya does once it hands off the lead to sales.

But is this a revolutionary story? Is "discovering, qualifying, and capturing sales" a radical new idea? Or is this use of Twitter an exciting phase of a natural *evolution*? Avaya's strategy seems like a logical next step—one that takes advantage of customers' enhanced connectivity, interactivity, and mobility. Doesn't it?

Avaya sells off the hook because it's keeping its eye on the prize. No matter what technology emerges next, it never loses track of priorities. When a new digital tool arrives, team members take a breath and evaluate it. First, Avaya decides if there's a way to make the tool serve a specific business need. Is it practical? Then it acts. Avaya succeeds because it evolves, but also because the company plans rather than hastily reacting.

A Better Way to Sell, Not Advertise

It's important to take notice of what's working for savvy companies like Avaya and apply it. These winners thrive because they're keeping perspective and evolving. They're focusing on planning *practical* processes that reach *beyond* grabbing customers' attention, beyond advertising.

Think back to Logan Services from chapter 1. Is Amanda Kinsella's secret sauce rooted in how often she Tweets, how often she updates Facebook, or how entertaining she is? Is Marcus Sheridan funnier, "more human," or better at communicating an irreverent brand image than his competitors? Or is success being born of a more practical formula? Is selling more, more often, having *more* to do with the stuff we already understand and are good at? Might success have *less* to do with new ideas like social graphs?

In our haste to evolve marketing, many of us are using social media to do something very familiar: advertise. We're working to create awareness. Sadly, sales are often left to chance. After all, that's what mass media advertising is all about. And advertising is certainly practical. But is pushing messages outward on social media evolutionary? Does it take *full* advantage of the Web's interactivity?

The people calling the shots at exceptional companies like Avaya are having more profitable interactions with customers, more often because social media is their new tool to exchange value with customers, intimately. And they're doing that in super-relevant ways based on customers' need at that precise moment. Social technology is a logical, evolutionary step. Hey, isn't that a different, *refreshing perspective* on the opportunity? This way, social media marketing becomes more than a new way to gain attention; it represents a better way to sell.

Publish More, Advertise Less, Win More Sales

The successful businesses profiled in this book are publishing various flavors of informational utilities. They're providing customers with a *qualitatively better* experience with products or services. They're evolving—putting their businesses in extraordinarily good positions to listen, translate, and build unique levels of trust with customers. But they're also gaining new customers *at reduced advertising cost*. Now that's an evolutionary step that most businesses can appreciate.

For instance, if you read HubSpot's blog, you'll quickly notice that the company enjoys talking about how little pay-per-click search engine advertising it invests in. From CEO Brian Halligan on down, HubSpotters are quick to point out that many of their customers report doing the same—once they start blogging, for instance. This company and its growing stable of customers challenges a popular notion. That is, the smartest thing a business can do with Google is advertise on it. Other like-minded businesses agree. They're discovering how the "non-advertising" side of search engines is a better place to get discovered and to become *trusted* by potential customers and ultimately earn the sale.

"People think of blogging as a search engine optimization tool. That's such a minor component of it," says small business owner Marcus Sheridan. "And sure, it's great to get lots of visits. I love that. But it's even better to gain *trust* and *close sales* using content."

Sheridan is one HubSpot customer that can tell motivational and insightful stories. For instance, one day he had an appointment with a woman he met two years prior. Back then, she didn't buy from Sheridan. She wasn't ready. But he *this time* she announced her willingness to invest. This confirmed one of Sheridan's suspicions. So before leaving the office that day, he checked his blog management software. Sure enough, he noticed a rise in Web pages his prospect was viewing on his blog.

"Within the first five minutes of conversation (at her house) I told her, 'Dawn, I let you slip through the cracks two years ago, but I'm not going to do that again today,'" recounts Sheridan, who says the woman laughed off his comment.

But he was quite serious. And after going through routine sales processes, he gave his prospect the price. Dawn said it was a good one, but also that she was "not ready to decide today."

"But then she told me, 'Well, to be honest, I have another appointment for a quote.' In fact, she had three appointments," says Sheridan.

He quickly thought to himself: (1) This prospect had subscribed to his blog two years prior, (2) she demonstrated to him, that day, that she read all of his blogs for the last two years, and (3) she was educated enough to finish many of his sentences during the visit! She openly admitted his blog was the source of all her knowledge on fiberglass pools.

Sheridan confidently responded. He said, "'Dawn, this competitor you're about to meet with. How many articles have they sent you over the last two years that have taught you about pools?'"

"She said 'none.'"

"I then asked her, 'How many times have they given you something that was really, really insightful—that, whether you bought a pool from them or not, was helping you with this decision?'"

"She said, 'Well ... none.'"

"I said, 'How many times have I sent you, over these last two years, Dawn, something of value that's helping you make this decision?' She said, 'I guess hundreds of articles.'"

"'That's right,' I said. I then said to her, 'The reality is that you actually want to get this pool from us, don't you? Simply because we've given you more than anyone else. We care about you. So my question is if we care so much about you, and you're now so much smarter thanks to our blog, why are you getting more quotes?'"

"To make a long story short, she said, 'You're right, I don't even know why. I just want to get two or three quotes like everyone says I should.' And that was it. It was done. She gave me a deposit, and she was so relieved. But that only occurred because of content," says Sheridan. "Content is the key to developing that trust over time."

And that's the very practical reason why Marcus Sheridan is **evolving** his business—investing less in advertising and more in publishing. Blogging and publishing educational videos puts River Pools and Spas in the best position to gain the trust of prospects and close more sales. Is Sheridan controversial? Wildly so. Does he have a flamboyant character, unique voice, and all that jazz? You bet. But he sells off the hook because his eye is on the prize, he works hard, **makes content work hard for him**, and asks for the sale. No matter what technology emerges next, he never loses track of his priority: selling. His pool business thrives when others struggle to break even because Sheridan **evolves** with the times.

It's true stories like this that make me stop and say, "But what about 'the social media revolution?'" Marcus Sheridan just flies in the face of what we hear so much of these days from "experts." When sales rise, social media is quick to step up and take credit. But when sales fall, it must be the customers' fault— they're not buying! Of course, many "experts" consider it blasphemous to speak of selling using social media. But these people aren't the real deal. They're not my hero. Marcus Sheridan is my guy, and I'll bet he's growing on you, too. He's a real salesman, putting social media to work for his company in really *practical* ways. He's a true, one-of-a-kind, rare breed of social media marketing expert.

On Experts

"Every time there is a sizable shift in the way businesses communicate with consumers, there is always a cadre of 'experts' ... people that advise that a new business paradigm has arrived," says Allan Dick, COO of Mountaintop, Pennsylvania-based Vintage Tub and Bath. "One in which traditional theories of running a business get thrown out the door. What these experts miss is that the theories remain the same. It's the ways you execute those theories that change."

Dick asks us to remember back to the whole "just get eyeballs to your Web site and the profits will come" mania of the early 2000s.

"Common sense took a holiday," says Dick, who offers us an example of what he means. In 1916, long before the digital age was even an idea, Leon L. Bean posted this notice on the front door of his store: "I do not consider a sale completed until goods are worn out and the customer is still satisfied."

"Brilliant in its simplicity," says Dick. "The advent of radio, television, mass media, and the Internet—these are simply *new ways* to make certain the customer is still satisfied. It is not a replacement or alternative to taking care of the customer or standing behind your products. It is not some great mystery that requires self-anointed pundits to climb the magic mountain to gain some new nugget of wisdom and bestow it upon unenlightened businesses."

Dick would know. He's built a successful business by taking his own medicine. As he puts it, "Caring for your customers, watching your expenses, and genuinely partnering with everyone that touches your business. Profits will usually follow. Everything else is either commentary that explains this concept or it is useless noise to be rigorously avoided."

Evaluate, Redefine the Opportunity

Allan Dick is on to something because I'm finding a single commonality between social marketers who sell successfully: the way they're viewing the opportunity itself. A unique, traditional business perspective drives how they're addressing the challenge standing before them. Companies like Avaya see social media as a chance to help do what they're already doing, but better. They're focused on adapting new social marketing tools to the fundamentals of their business—*not the other way around!* They're not buying into the revolutionary hype.

> *Successful social sellers use social media to help improve what they're already doing. They're focused on adapting new social marketing tools to the fundamentals of their business—not the other way around! They're not buying into the revolutionary hype.*

Specifically, companies that sell off the hook feel compelled to *qualify* the opportunity standing before them first. They aren't feeling burdened or rushed by social media's arrival. They don't feel like they need to be on Twitter, LinkedIn, and Facebook. Yes, customers are there now. But their instinct is to *evaluate*—find out *if* being in those spaces is worthwhile at all. If social media is deemed opportunistic enough, they invest time in fully understanding *why*.

Make no mistake, exceptional companies like Avaya, Logan Services, and Vintage Tub are eager to evaluate how social tools might help achieve business goals. But their first instinct is not to do. Rather, it is to *ask questions*—better questions.

"Wondering what an organization's social media strategy should be is very much the same as wondering about what its telephone strategy would be: It is the wrong question," says Olivier Blanchard of BrandBuilder Marketing.

For instance, what if Bigelow's team had not reacted so quickly to the notion of informative YouTube videos that go viral? What if they had simply asked, "Why is that a good idea?" Under this approach, might Bigelow have been more aware of the chance to *sell tea* using YouTube? Through a slightly more thoughtful lens, the company's management team may have been less excited at the idea of generating attention with YouTube, thus opening the door to consider other, more important options—like selling.

It seems that most of us are *reacting* to the social Web's arrival. We're a bit jumpy and looking for a quick answer. Hey, we're only human! But when we're in a less reactionary mode, we tend to ask ourselves the more important questions. Priorities snap into focus. Think of it this way: If Bigelow's team were less inclined to just do it (react), they might have asked their agency, "What if we give YouTube viewers a reason to *interact* with the company as part of the campaign? This could give us the chance to understand more about viewers—reach beyond educating them or getting Bigelow's name out there."

Someone may have cooked up a practical idea like mixing in a sweepstakes, contest, or promotion of some kind. Bigelow could have given away something valuable as an ethical bribe of sorts in exchange for a chance to collect insight on the viewer. For instance, the video could have made a call to action that drove viewers to a short Web form at Bigelow.com/sweeps. The company could discover who viewers are (an e-mail address) and the kind of teas they enjoy drinking.

By designing the YouTube video to capture qualitative information about individual viewers, Bigelow could have created an e-mail list of qualified prospects. This way, Bigelow could continually build the list and exploit it more fully using promotions that entice customers toward purchase. In this scenario, the tea giant would ultimately have a way to tie resulting sales directly to the YouTube campaign, and probably a good means to optimize those sales, too.

As we'll continue to discover, today's best social sellers are instinctively *evaluating*, not rushing in and doing. They're taking a breath and redefining the opportunity itself by qualifying social media. They *are* enthusiastically jumping in to apply social tools, but they're doing so thoughtfully and only when they can serve a mature purpose.

Making Video Sell to New Customers

For instance, Tractor Supply Company (TSC) is the largest retail farm and ranch store chain in America with $3 billion in sales and 15,000 employees. This popular rural lifestyle retailer has been providing basic maintenance products to rural farmers, "hobby farmers," and ranchers since 1938. And like Avaya, TSC is *evolving* in ways that use video to sell off the hook. But what is TSC's social media approach rooted in, and how does a business built on such traditional, old-fashioned values decide when, where, why, and how to venture into social media?

Traditionally, TSC sells everything from welders and generators to animal care products to work wear for men and women. They sell practical things like pet supplies, animal feed, power tools, riding mowers, and lawn and garden products. But a handful of trends are combining to create a new, emerging market for TSC. Namely the organic, slow food, and local food ("localvore") movements have combined with urban flight to explode TSC's potential market. More and more, urban dwellers want to know (intimately) what they're eating, and they're turning to small farmers for food or wanting to *become* weekend farmers themselves.

According to Andrew Heltsley, TSC's marketing manager, this is creating a sizable opportunity to sell his products, but, he says, *only* if this new market has *the right knowledge*. So the company is giving early-adopter customers the confidence, understanding, and actual know-how needed to succeed, and they're delivering it to customers using new tools like social media.

TSC realizes it cannot sell into this new market without investing in it. But then again, TSC has been practicing custom publishing for decades. Fostering demand among customers with knowledge isn't a radical, new concept. Witness the company's *Out Here* magazine (www.oth.me/tracsup). It features tips and tricks on everything from yummy recipes to raising rare livestock and horses. TSC has been helping customers *get things done* better, smarter, and faster since the beginning.

Today, TSC's online *Know How Central* (www.oth.me/tscknowhow) is a treasure trove of how-to knowledge from how to choose tools (like generators or welders) to solar-powered home improvement. Need help with hay-harvesting basics, buying the right trailer, pet care advice, chain saw tips, or feeding sheep, goats, and rabbits? TSC's *Know How Central* can help.

For instance, one of today's hottest trends is raising chickens in more population-dense areas. But how? TSC is using online video to educate and exploit an explosive "backyard chicken" market. The company is reaching into uncharted territory—educating city folk in more metropolitan areas. And they're doing it with a step-by-step how-to on raising chickens. To accomplish this, Heltsley and his team are partnering with Andy Schneider, the host of *The Backyard Poultry with the Chicken Whisperer* Web radio show. Schneider's successful, tips-focused show caught TSC's interest given the priority on chicken (www.oth.me/chicktips).

Heltsley is rolling out a complete educational video series designed to nurture this budding new market. His reasoning and approach are simple: Stick to your knitting. Do what you know works. For Heltsley, that means keep giving potential TSC customers the know-how needed to buy products. He's not entertaining them with funny chicken videos or cheap, flashy gimmicks. Is this a revolutionary story, or is TSC simply evolving—applying its existing know-how to take advantage of a new medium? TSC's strategy is a logical next step. This retailer is selling off the hook because it hasn't lost track of the goal: to sell. No matter what technology emerges next, TSC never loses track of priorities.

Make Sales, Not Branding

What happens when we do lose track, when we buy into the revolution? We sometimes hear words like, "Yes, we didn't generate the leads we had anticipated, but now a lot of people know our brand. We got some 'good branding' from the investment."

For instance, a few years ago, IBM needed leads for its large, expensive mainframe computers. Similar to Bigelow's experience, "experts" told Big Blue leads would materialize from viral buzz resulting from a YouTube video. The idea for *Mainframe: The Art of the Sale* was born. The idea was for IBM to broadcast absurd stories about its sales force on YouTube. You're probably familiar with the popular "humiliate yourself—people love it and you'll look more human" idea. Well, IBM was sold on the idea of humorous conversation that goes viral. This, guru wisdom dictates, is effective at generating sales.

Although IBM did get some attention, few leads could be attributed to the wacky video series. But then again, the videos were not designed to elicit a *behavior* from viewers. For instance, they didn't direct prospects to visit a Web site, call a phone number, or take some kind of action. Of course, the campaign was dubbed a big win. At least, so say the experts who created it. But they didn't blindly attribute leads to their efforts. They couldn't. By their own admission, it was a success because tens of thousands of viewers clicked the video play button. It got some attention.

The goal switched. Suddenly, IBM was *not* after sales leads—it was *really* looking for views on a video player. It was looking for attention, not leads.

When all else fails, people sometimes put lipstick on the pig. Maybe you've heard it within the walls of your business when a tradeshow or marketing campaign under delivers. "Yes, we didn't generate the leads we had anticipated, but now a lot of people know our brand." But what if IBM had honestly *expected more* out of their foray into social media to begin with? Might they have *designed* videos to prompt viewer behavior beyond hoping people laugh? Would IBM's team have designed a way to identify who the viewer was and *where they were in the purchase process*?

"Talking isn't a big new idea; rather, many of us have mistakenly redefined its purpose to be entertaining, engaging, and to sell nothing," warns author and branding consultant Jonathan Salem Baskin.

By simply prompting viewer response (beyond laughing and sharing), IBM could have developed a qualified list of *leads* through its YouTube campaign. Big Blue's investment in the videos could have been funny *and* profitable.

Make It Quality Time, Not a Pastime

Good social marketing strategies give your businesses knowledge—a clear understanding of where a customer is at in the purchase or repurchase process, for instance. And they give customers useful, satisfying answers. Pretty simple. So where does humor fit in?

> *Good social marketing strategies provide a clear view of where a given customer is within the purchase decision process, not just a momentary laugh or feel-good.*

Let's consider: do customers yearn for businesses to share in their sadness or happiness through corporate consciousness, or would they rather have a business present solutions to problems in their lives—fulfill their needs? Often times experts tell us that social media is our big chance to be perceived as "more human" or that customers want our businesses to make them laugh. But do they want a good yuk *as much or more* than they want to be understood, advised, or satisfied? Might they want *quality time* more than a pastime?

For instance, let's contrast Adagio's successful use of social media (it's "tea timer," chapter 4) with that of Sweden-based Ikea. The global home goods retailer was opening a new European store, and store management decided to use Facebook in a way that spread its product images far and wide across the social network. This, Ikea believed, would be a good way to use Facebook to promote its store opening. Through product images, it would become more known to Facebook users.

The end result was heralded as a huge success by Web marketing trade media, bloggers, and gurus, but it it provided little value to Ikea beyond a massive display of product images across Facebook pages. Ikea failed to discover and nurture demand or prompt useful customer behavior, as Adagio's tea timer does. Neither did it serve a useful *purpose* with Facebook users.

Ikea's idea was to give away a handful of store items. In return, those products would be seen virally as widely and as often as possible across Facebook. Product images were uploaded as photos within a Facebook profile Ikea's new store created. Upon seeing a product image, any Facebook user could "tag" the image (associate themselves with it) and win it. First come, first served. But was this quality time with prospective customers?

The campaign was not part of a larger system of prompts that "kept customers moving along" toward a preconceived result, and the behavior Ikea induced was sharing photos, not a series of gestures moving customers toward buying.

But what if Ikea took its photo-tagging concept and focused on a market segment important to that particular store, and what if they added an element that discovered more about that segment's needs? For instance, the store could have traded the chance to win free stuff for a bit of insightful information about a specific customer group as a requirement to participate. In doing so, Ikea would have developed a prospecting database for future follow-up.

As an example, incoming or first-year college students are prime targets for Ikea's contemporary, cost-effective, and lightweight furniture. By identifying contest participants who were students, the company could have developed a

targeted follow up e-mail campaign or a Facebook communications routine—
something geared to prompt store visits through any number of student-focused
promotions.

Alternatively, Ikea could have offered the chance to win something in
exchange for the chance to solve problems or make life easier for students. "How
to Design Your Dorm" video programs, articles, or an interactive application
could have been provided—preloaded with stylish tips geared for young men or
women. Content could be delivered in whatever format the audience chooses—
articles, e-newsletters, podcasts, or short video programs. Each piece of content
would be designed to foster demand for Ikea's products. Calls to action, promotions, and so on may be sprinkled in to induce an exchange of information
between Ikea and prospects. Getting this done is as simple as asking contest
participants to identify themselves and choose a problem to have Ikea solve. By
segmenting male and female students, the tips, tricks, and valuable content can
be tailored by typical, gender-driven needs, goals, and interests.

In addition to giving students a chance to win products, Ikea could have
improved the lives of future buyers today and nurtured relationships toward
sales transactions tomorrow. This kind of quality-time thinking would have
given Ikea's team something to work with long term when courting customers.
Instead, the store settled for a flash-in-the-pan Facebook campaign.

But to be fair, Ikea, IBM, and Bigelow's first forays into social media were
like many these days—aimed at creating awareness. They were campaigns which
may or may not have caused a sale. We'll never know, and that's a shame. But
don't get me wrong. The marketing and advertising teams at these companies
were then—and are today—diligently trying to make social media pay them
back in real dollars, and they're certainly not stupid. The fact is that most of
us fail to sell because we're distracted, losing track of the real goal: sales. We're
falling back on branding awareness.

What about your business? Could you or those who work for you be letting
enthusiasm for social media distract from the real goal? Are you taking the time
to *qualify* specific opportunities social media provides before taking action?
When acting, are you creating *purposeful* quality time with customers?

Be Social, Don't "Do" It

The authors of *Cluetrain Manifesto* (www.cluetrain.org) were right: markets are conversations. Companies like Avaya, Logan Services, and Tractor Supply Company and others are living proof of the concept. But if social media gives us the chance to converse with more customers more often, why aren't most businesses having dialogues that lead to sales more frequently?

"If your company culture doesn't focus on building relationships with your customers, then chances are that you won't use social media to do it either. The 'media' doesn't dictate how social a company is or isn't. It simply enhances its ability to be a social business—if in fact it is. If not, it illustrates the extent to which it isn't," says Olivier Blanchard of BrandBuilder Marketing.

Indeed, selling off the hook takes tact. But hasn't it always? And how does this explain why more of us are not delicately, yet deliberately, conversing in ways that guide customers toward destinations they choose? Blanchard makes a powerful point.

"'Social' is something you *are*, not something you *do*," he says.

While it seems obvious, has it been forgotten? In all the excitement around the promise of social media, people may be overlooking a critical fact: The conversational element powering online commerce is *not* new. In fact, it dates back to the beginning of civilized trade, but that's not what we hear from overzealous social media enthusiasts and charlatans.

"This idea that conversation is a new experience and that it has an innate value is simply incorrect. It doesn't. It never did," says author, speaker, and leading branding consultant Jonathan Salem Baskin.

Baskin says the definition of conversation many businesses are adopting is largely nonsense espoused by gurus. That is, conversation is a new, automatically valuable tool for marketers. Baskin believes this definition is disingenuous, false hyperbole—not valuable wisdom. He reminds us how businesses have been conversing with customers, vendors, suppliers, and critics since the beginning.

"When we talk about social experience, we're talking about civilization," says Baskin. "And people within civilizations have been talking to, at, and about one another since time began."

Baskin, whose book *Histories of Social Media* (www.oth.me/socialhistory)

dives deeply into this subject, believes many businesses are right to enthusiastically adopt new social communications tools. But he warns that too many are looking at customer conversations in a vacuum and not looking at them as an on-going experience.

"I mean, brands in the fifties had conversations with their customers. Now we might laugh at them," says Baskin. "But they *did* have conversations. They told the market things; the market shared things; people referred things; they recommended; the market pushed back. Again, we can laugh and say that they were, in effect, cave men and women trying to conduct business. But there *were* conversations going on."

"These days, we scoff at the substance of those dialogues, but they told people things that had meaning, relevance, and prompted sales, and thereby built most of the big names we can cite today," says Baskin.

As it turns out "social" is something you *are*, not something you *do*. But more importantly, Baskin says affirming that the conversation is *not* new will improve your business's ability to realize benefits from social media.

For instance, consider how socially driven realtors are. They're hyperdependent on being able to master emotionally driven conversation—win friends and influence people. And they're in a power position to affirm and experience more success using social media because realtors *already have* the proven, effective strategies. They have the essential social business skills needed to succeed.

Hey, should realtors be schooling social media experts? After all, realtors are the ones who've mastered profiting from the use of social constructs. Who better to apply marketing within social media than realtors themselves?

The History of Social Media

Think back to the early- to- mid-1990s. The World Wide Web was just arriving. If you were lucky, your business would be disrupted. But if not, you were to be disintermediated—bypassed altogether. Killed off. Your entire business was a worthless middle-tier of fat that needed to be cut out. And if you'll recall, two professions were as-good-as-dead: travel and real estate agents. Today, sites like Expedia, Travelocity, Trulia.com and Zillow.com are still around. But, lo! So are realtors.

As it turns out, the mountain of real estate data being given to home buyers isn't terribly valuable by itself. What is? The interpreters: realtors. And that's how it's always been. Sure, opinions and knowledge-sharing on the Web ("the wisdom of crowds") is helpful. But it's *not* always trusted or valued. In fact, an increasing amount of research dismantles the idea that crowds are good at helping individuals make better—or even good—decisions. For instance, in 1985, Garold Stasser and William Titus published striking research in the *Journal of Personality and Social Psychology*. They found that people trying to make decisions in groups spend most of the time telling each other things that everyone already knows. In other words, groups of people are *unlikely* to bring up new information known only to themselves. The result: poor decisions.

In the end, buyers and sellers still value working with knowledgeable, credentialed people like realtors more than "the crowd." After all the hype and spin, trust and critical thinking matter more to people.

Today, realtors clearly have social business know-how, given their expertise in conducting conversations that lead to consumer trust, for instance. Realtors simply need to pick and choose from an array of new digital marketing tools. They *already know* how to apply them. Again, is your business any different? And with all this "looking forward," should we actually be *getting back to our roots—* exploiting what we already know about what works?

"If you strip away the technology, you open up a rich resource of case histories that better explain the dynamics, shortcomings, and immense opportunities for social media," says Jonathan Salem Baskin, whose book analyzes two thousand years of history to uncover tips for today's work with social media.

The Power of Purpose

In essence, true experts like Olivier Blanchard and Jonathan Salem Baskin want us to free ourselves because it makes practical sense. Unshackling your business from misguided ideas of gurus empowers you to define clear, process-driven *purposes* for social media projects. You'll discover mature reasons for starting and participating in meaningful conversations—social media-powered discussions that ultimately sell off the hook.

For instance, consider how many of your customers want to be the first to know about new products or services. This is just one example of a *mature business purpose* social media can serve in the lives of customers. For instance, Heather Gorringe of UK-based Wiggly Wigglers (www.wigglywigglers.com) is always finding new ways to tip off her gardening customers on exciting, new, niche products using Facebook, blogs, podcasts, and video. She's prompting discussions with customers—chats about solutions to problems—and she's doing it often before her customers even know they have a problem! What a fine gesture that serves a useful, mutually beneficial *purpose*.

"A lot of social campaigns that marketers do these days celebrate the idea of engagement, for instance, as being an absolute good thing. They've concluded this because we're able to converse with people, and conversing with them is (inherently) good. They admit that *what* we actually converse about is important. But (in practice) *what* we're talking about is becoming secondary to this 'new' tool that we've discovered called conversation," says a concerned Baskin.

Designing digital conversations in ways that produce meaningful, relevant experiences for customers (and profits for businesses) doesn't just happen. It demands relevance and purpose, he says.

Keith Wiegold, adjunct professor at Northwestern University and founder of engagement marketing company Nutlug agrees and reminds us of the role played by context. He sees many marketers rushing to measure buzz and engagement in ways that do not connect with the where and why driving customers' shopping behavior.

"The definition of engagement is undefined. And measurement is therefore uncertain and generally misguided. Many current efforts look at what a marketer is doing to 'be engaging' (breadth or depth of social media, content efforts, and so on) without asking the sole determiners of whether they are 'engaged'—the customers themselves," says Wiegold. "Any measurement around engagement must be customer-based. It must take into consideration that what engagement means changes based on where the customer is at throughout their journey with the brand."

Many of the businesses in this book are starting relevant, meaningful, and purpose-driven conversations—those that are worth having. They know whom to converse with, how, and why, and they're *behaving* (conversing) in ways that generate continuous customer responses—behaviors that produce leads and sales.

Think about being social in terms of your business. Are you eliciting problems from customers so you can talk to them about the answers? Doesn't this kind of idea play a more powerful role than merely getting customers' attention?

"Purposeful conversation has outcomes, implications, and requirements," says Jonathan Salem Baskin. "If you think about it, the things that define conversation have mattered throughout all of history. If we don't have outcomes and requirements as part of our marketing conversation, we're kinda just wasting everyone's time. And I think that might be why we're experiencing some trouble finding measures and metrics that are believable, sustainable, and realistic."

"So, again, I get back to this idea that we look at conversation now as if it's an absolute good. And I don't think it is," says Baskin, who warns that marketers need to get busy finding a higher purpose for social marketing programs.

You Already Have the Answers

And where do we find that higher purpose? Let's start with a question. What if you started putting more stock in *existing* knowledge and abilities? This theme runs throughout most of the success stories in this book and continues on www .jeffmolander.com/blog and www.offthehookblog.com. Gaining confidence in traditional strengths is a reliable way to convert daunting challenges into very doable opportunities.

And here's the exciting part: digging deep into your heart and mind can produce measurable improvements to sales, but only if we agree on a new idea: The social Web has not upended fundamental laws of business. Assuming this perspective will empower you because this new, more realistic viewpoint shines a bright light on the truth: your business probably already has most of the answers it needs in hand. In other words, marketing isn't being reinvented. That's just hype. We're just being given the chance to *adapt* it, to *improve* it, to help it evolve and better serve us.

Let's take a quick, real-life look at what happens when a stores-based retailer assumes this new perspective. Adrian Taylor Junior and Adrian Senior operate two Ben Franklin craft stores (www.bfranklincrafts.com) in rural Washington, and they've been doing it for two decades. I met the two businessmen at a convention after a speaking engagement. The father–son duo had missed my speech and were seeking guidance from someone whom they perceived to be an expert, but it was I who received the schooling!

In the face of a historic economic recession, holiday season 2009 was the Taylor's biggest ever. I say again, the biggest ever. Needless to say, I jumped— asked them how they did it. They mentioned how a charitable idea "went viral" in their community thanks to a simple "giving tree" promotion during holiday season. Ornaments hanging on a window-front holiday tree featured children of local, incarcerated parents. Children asked not for toys; but underwear, shoes, basic necessities. The lists were heartbreaking, and community folk flooded into the store upon hearing word. Many made cash donations and, while they were there, shopped for the holidays. This very "analog" (non-digital) idea obviously worked on multiple levels. It provided the gift of giving to donors, encouraged shopping, and put basic necessities into the hands of some of the neediest kids.

Before I could explain to these gentlemen that they *already understood* "the secret sauce," Adrian Jr. had an epiphany. He had donated to the Red Cross Haiti relief effort in Spring 2010. Suddenly, Adrian Jr. realized how digital marketing could be applied in a way that could multiply the success of his future charitable events.

Adrian Jr. had SMS-text-messaged his relief donation. A week or so afterward, he received a SMS message back. The Red Cross ship was pulling into port and unloading needed goods. The moment deeply moved him and "closed the loop" on his kind gesture. He explained to me how that experience gave him the urge to take more, similar actions.

The experience affirmed Adrian Jr.'s realization that digital tools are cool. Really cool. But they're not creating new meaning in customers' lives so much as they are allowing deeply meaningful events to happen in new ways, more often, instantly and anywhere. The real success factor in his store promotion—and in the Haiti relief effort—was fostering a meaningful experience for people. A bell went off in his head. Adrian Jr. realized that digital tools like mobile SMS and e-mail are most effective when supporting *what he and his father already knew works*. Everything else is gratuitous. A well-designed, meaningful experience is what works. He knew that to be certain because it's what has *always* worked.

Adrian Jr. began to plan. He would use SMS text messaging in his next in-store charitable campaign just as the Red Cross did. He would use it in ways that induce and reward behavior, and his store, charity, and customers would all benefit. Adrian Jr.'s "ah-ha" was that mobile, social media merely gives his store a new communication tool. The tools themselves aren't revolutionary, complex, or able to produce meaningful events on their own. They're just new. They may or may not apply to a particular goal. That decision was his.

Yes, these tools often get customers attention and engagement. But smart marketers like Adrian Jr. are starting to realize that attention is just the first step in a *larger process*. Ironically, this idea was precisely what my message was in the lecture that day. To their surprise, Adrian Jr. and Sr. had missed nothing. They were already on the right path to using social media technologies in purposeful, profitable ways. They just needed affirmation.

Amanda Kinsella of HVAC business, Logan-Services (chapter 1), had the same "ah-ha" moment and is reaping the benefits ever since.

"Social media gives us the chance to take what we already know works and crank up the volume," says Kinsella, who knows better than to reinvent the wheel.

"For instance, acting as a resource center to customers and prospects is what we spend most of our time doing at home improvement shows. Social media just gives us a better set of tools to work with—a better way to do what we've always been doing for customers. Being a problem-solving resource as a way to earn customer relationships is core to how we've always done business," she says.

The path toward giving your social programs higher purpose is paved by a new perspective, one where the social media opportunity is framed as a practical, hype-free evolution where social media serves you and where your success is built on a foundation of what already works. Bold innovators like Debbie Qaqish call this brave new world "revenue marketing."

"This is going to be the year of the revenue marketer," says Qaqish. "Now you have to understand what I mean when I use the term revenue marketer. It's the marketer that has a repeatable, predictable, and sustainable practice for impacting top-line revenue growth in a company—not someone just executing campaigns."

Again, as you take action in your business life, consider this question on a day-to-day basis. Maybe hang it on the wall: Are you *using* social media tools or *designing* interactions with customers in ways that sell, in ways that earn repeatable, predictable, and sustainable revenue? There's a big difference.

Reflection questions:

1. Has instantaneous, ubiquitous digital communications (via social media) created new power for customers? Or is it actually *amplifying* their *existing* power? What does that mean in terms of how you're using social media marketing today? What change on day-to-day activities and campaigns might this realization force you to consider? Using this new context, how can you make better decisions that create more leads and sales?

2. Find purpose. What are the business outcomes you need from social media marketing? What are the outcomes currently being produced? As an example, you might identify awareness (marketing goal) and sales (business objective) or buzz (marketing goal) and leads (business objective). Write them down side by side. Try to connect marketing goals with business outcomes based on the results you're seeing today. This exercise will give insight on how purpose-driven your social media marketing efforts are.

3. Who's your daddy? Do you follow gurus and trends or customers? Call a meeting to get better insight on how your marketing team makes decisions. Flying solo? No worries, just introspect. Look for patterns. How often do you or your team look inward (i.e., at customers; at patterns in behavior) versus externally (i.e., gurus, experts, consultants) for guidance?

4. Define success as *sales*. What are your top two most successful social media marketing campaigns to date? Write them down. Now examine outcomes they produced in a strict business context. In other words, which of the successful campaigns created measurable increases in sales, leads, customer loyalty, or other tangible improvements in products and services or business processes that tie to sales? Once you've identified the two events, ask yourself, "Do each of these successes still deserve the 'success' label?"

5. Zero in on what works. Consider Andrew Heltsley's story. In particular, focus on his realization that what's always worked offline is what will work online. Has your organization experienced a similar "learning?" Pick a non-Web marketing campaign that really worked. Then consider how a digital tool or experience could help create more and improved outcomes. Put together a thumbnail sketch of why and how it would prompt purpose-driven behavior.

CHAPTER 5

AVOIDING THE
INFLUENCE TRAP

*"Influence in the mass media space
no longer fits the traditional marketing and
advertising model because mass media itself
is no longer a top-down model."*

*Olivier Blanchard,
BrandBuilder Marketing*

INFLUENCE. It's what social media gurus say your company should be pursuing. "Influencing the influencers" is the Holy Grail. It's the key to unlocking leads and sales using social media. But could behavior be a more practical tool? Might all the hype about influencers be a trap?

Rachel Happe is an independent social media consultant who believes the movement to measure and control top-down influence misses the mark. That is, it emphasizes the idea that one person alone is influential or "on top." She says focusing on top, individual influencers to talk about your product is actually **counterproductive**. It relies on rather flimsy theory.

Olivier Blanchard of BrandBuilder Marketing thinks likewise but goes further, questioning the very foundation that the "influencing the influencer" theory is based on. He agrees Kim Kardashian, Leighton Meester, and Justin Bieber help sell whatever they get photographed wearing. Drew Barrymore and Queen Latifah sell makeup. Leonardo DiCaprio sells Tag Heuer watches. Yes, "top-down" or "mass" influencers are real, and how top-down influence works is scientifically documented and relevant in the world of big advertising and Madison Avenue.

"But this type of influence is now increasingly limited and narrow in scope and not immediately relevant when applied to complex, real-time, laterally driven social networks," concludes Blanchard. He believes influencers can be found within the masses, not just at the top of their respective subcultural family trees, and he backs up the assertion that influence is not a "top-down" phenomenon.

"*Urban* fashions didn't start on a runway in New York or Milan," says Blanchard, who agrees with Happe. "'Gangsta' culture wasn't designed in a Soho creative studio and then packaged and sold to rap superstars. It came from the street and was *then* commercialized."

Blanchard says these same bottom-up and lateral mechanisms are "true of punk rock, skateboarding, surfing, and just about every 'culture' or 'subculture' you can throw a cat at, from triathlons, to amateur photography, to the country-club lifestyle. Influence starts at the bottom, not at the top."

"There are so many discussions lately of what makes a person and influencer, and a lot of people and brands are swarming around the people they have determined to be influential," says Rachel Happe, who blogs at www.thesocial organization.com. "And it's not completely wrong, but influence is so much more complex than that."

Happe says the social media industry is oversimplifying by pushing the theory of a single, ultra-influential person having a significant effect on behavior of others in their network.

"That is rarely the case," she says. "When making a judgment about something, people rarely hear about it from one (influential) person and then go buy or consume it. The process is more like this: they become aware of it through a whole variety of ways—media, friends, advertisements—and then they might hear a friend mention it. Then they hear someone else talking about it. Then they take a closer look. Then they ask someone and do some research. Then they might not do anything for a bit. Then a need arises, and they go do something about it. Now, tell me who was the 'influencer' that caused them to take action? The truth is, it was no one person alone."

> *Pushing individual influencers to talk about your thing more is actually counterproductive.*
> *Rather, prompt behavior among the entire network of inputs that surround them. Create a "flow of influence."*

Instead, Happe suggests it usually takes a network and a "flow of influence" to create action. Of course, it is difficult to tell which part of that flow has the most influence on the individual taking action. But she says there's yet another paradox: the more one individual influencer pushes something, the more their recommendation gets called into question because it often looks (and is) biased in some way.

"So pushing individual influencers to talk about your thing more is actually counterproductive," Happe warns.

So what is more effective? Happe says if you are trying to get a customer or prospect to take action, you should prompt behavior among the entire network of inputs that surround them. It is just as important (perhaps more so) to get the "second, third, and fourth-tier people" that are "around" someone to recommend a product as it is to get one person to do so. By prompting dense subnetworks of individuals to take an action, you can affect behavior more than by targeting hubs of multiple networks.

"After all, the popular girls are only popular if they have a posse," says Happe. "The posse matters a lot. Without their support, there would be no popular girls. Followers matter as much as leaders; we just forget that."

"We should be thinking about creating networks and flows of influence," advises Happe. "Not piling on to already overwhelmed influencers."

But how do we create networks and flows of influence, practically speaking?

With all this controversy over the origins of influence—and how to put it to work for our businesses—is influencing the influencers worth it, or is it a trap?

Behavior: A Practical Kind of Influence

Identify purchase decision makers and influence them. Persuade them. It's a familiar advertising idea. As nineteenth-century Danish philosopher Soren Kierkegaard said, "In order to save men's souls, one must first seduce them." Fair enough. Selling is courtship. This fact has stood the test of time, and it remains a useful, foundational idea powering successful, modern-day marketing communications programs—especially ad campaigns.

More recently, Malcolm Gladwell's *Tipping Point* has updated the age-old, fundamental ideas behind how influence works that people like Dale Carnegie popularized in the 1930s. Gladwell's version is a very sexy, popular marketing meme these days. But is the idea a practical tool for us or just a whiz-bang theory? Rachel Happe and Olivier Blanchard force us to consider serious questions.

How do we know influencing the influencers on the social Web works? If it does, how can we execute on this idea in ways that create results? More importantly, is the hype around complex ideas like "understanding customers' social graphs" distracting us from the real opportunity to make sales?

According to Greg Satell, SVP Strategy and Innovation at Moxie Interactive, "The problem with the network theory method (of turning influence into profitable outcomes) is that it's very difficult to implement, especially with large networks."

Satell, a statistician and math buff who blogs at digitaltonto.com, says this kind of theory is used in counterterrorism and organizational consulting. But even in a small network of, say, ten people, the number of statistical calculations is significant. Practicing this kind of science involves monitoring behavior across three "measures of influence" using the idea of "degree, betweenness, and closeness centrality." Heady stuff for sure. Satell says measuring across thousands or even millions of nodes makes the costs involved prohibitive for most businesses.

That's why large and small companies profiled in this book define influence in more practical terms, in ways they can act on today. For them, influence means the ability to *inspire meaningful and measurable action and outcomes* among customers. They define influence in terms they can control today.

For instance, every day at these companies, socially savvy marketers arrive at the office ready to induce actions. They use classic direct-response techniques to guide customers in ways that create mutual value. In fact, customers often guide themselves toward more products and services, more often. This is possible because the business is defining influence as something tangible: behavior.

For instance, in chapter 2, we discussed Disney and Burger King. Is Disney's Tickets Together program hard-selling movie tickets by blanketing Facebook with reminders to buy them? Is Burger King pounding away at reminding hungry people to buy their food in new and clever ways? Or are they simply helping existing customer demand become tangible, real in ways that benefit everyone involved? Might these companies be guiding customers toward destinations they (customers) have all but chosen—their products and services?

A handful of large brands and small businesses are quietly selling off the hook by redefining influence as being behaviorally-focused, and you can, too. If influence involves observable, moldable behavior, that means you can start making good things happen—again and again—today.

YouTube: Starting Conversations That Lead to Sales

For instance, global real estate firm Jones Lang LaSalle (JLL) is using social media to close leads on prospective and existing accounts more often. We touched on this firm in chapter 1, where we first met Gunnar Branson and considered the benefits of *provoking reactions* over trying to become a thought-leading business.

JLL uses short, insightful YouTube video clips (www.podcasts.joneslang lasalle.com) to motivate executive decision makers into action. As a result, they're inducing observable behavior that results in more closed leads, more often, all because they're communicating what the firms' experts are seeing and most clients are not. Specifically, trends and insights that reveal risk or opportunity.

JLL serves a handful of customers, including property owners. Clients are often businesses seeking commercial properties to buy. They may want to occupy them or rent them out. In any case, JLL's clients need advice on how to make their investments profitable, so JLL advises clients on how to invest, when, where, and why to actually help their clients get the job done—to make money in commercial real estate.

Like most businesses, JLL needs to be growing existing accounts by convincing current clients to sign on to other services, and that's one area where its YouTube videos are proving to be effective. They're worthwhile, productive conversations with clients. The company's team produces short, pointed, two- to four-minute video clips. JLL's client services team then distributes remarkably insightful tidbits to hand-picked clients. Each video short features a single expert providing candid, forward-thinking thoughts on global real estate trends. Before the Web arrived, these were the kinds of valuable opinions and research summaries clients typically paid to access. But today, JLL uses them as hooks.

For instance, one clip details exactly how New Zealand's industrial property market is staging a comeback (www.oth.me/joneslang). A JLL analyst ticks off a handful of surprising reasons why it may be time to consider investing. Another JLL video discusses the forthcoming economic recovery in the United Kingdom. The subject matter expert boldly states how unreliable most research is. Forecasting what to expect is nearly impossible. After all, the UK's economic troubles of the late 2000s were unprecedented. This in mind, JLL's video quickly summarizes what global economic history teaches investors as an alternative to unreliable predictions. An on-camera expert compares Sweden's economic turnaround to that of Japan's post-downturn recovery. The conclusion: the UK's recovery will likely look more like that of Sweden, based on recent governmental policy—political decisions that resemble those made by Sweden in years past.

Of course, if you're not a commercial real estate investor, such information isn't very influential. Heck, it's a bore. But for JLL's target market, it can be seriously provocative, and that's why JLL is constantly providing bold insights on what's around the corner for nervous, anxious clients. It's what they need, and that's influential to the point of creating measurable behavior.

Although the videos contain no explicit call to action, they prove remarkably effective at generating response because they're designed to. JLL's videos are high-touch tools used for calling on time-strapped, often emotionally driven clients, and they get strong reactions.

> *Videos are used surgically, delivered in*
> *personalized e-mail to prospects ... prompting them*
> *to quickly view and react.*
> *JLL's success is based on distribution (how),*
> *not just compelling messaging (what).*

The strategy works largely due to the content within the videos themselves but also due to how JLL's account team uses them. Videos are used surgically. They are not simply uploaded to YouTube with a hope that clients will discover them on search engines. The videos are optimized for search discovery, of course, and that's a possibility. But for JLL, the real opportunity lies in delivering videos to prospects within short e-mail messages, prompting clients to quickly view and react.

JLL is focused on process. The videos' length, substance, presentation, and style all weigh heavily into JLL's success. Subject matter experts are remarkably candid and believable. But distribution is key. Prospects are prompted to view videos in a personalized manner (a direct e-mail). JLL's strategy is successful because it's using short, compelling, relevant videos as a means to initiate conversations, but only those worth having. The firm's strategy is certainly to influence. But for JLL, influence is behavior: conversations that lead to mutually useful outcomes.

"The formula is something like this," says Gunnar Branson, "and it can be applied in any selling scenario: 'Most people think A, but it's actually B. Here's why I say that (so some sort of proof—an observation, trend, anecdote, a statistic). Therefore B.'"

"That's it," says Branson. "That's the way to plan or 'map out' stories or insights that will draw people in, that will establish far more than thought leadership. Because in today's business climate, thought leadership isn't based on your knowledge of what everyone else already knows. There is no shortage of articles, newsletters, white papers, and blogs that are essentially saying what everyone already knows and what everyone already agrees with.

"Instead, you're looking for what I jokingly call the sex and violence of business. That translates to opportunity and risk. Think about the things that always, naturally have people excited or worried. The rest is just finding an opportunity to discuss those things in a way that most people haven't seen yet. The goal is to examine a burning issue, trend, or something meaningful to customers in a slightly different way and along the way point out an opportunity or a risk that people need to think about. Both of those things—just like sex and violence in a movie—will draw people in, and they'll pay attention to you," says Branson.

"But from there, you're *not* trying to fully satisfy their appetite," he warns. "In other words, you're trying to make them hungry—trying to make that next step to call you, to write you, to e-mail you, to show up in your office to find out more about your products and services. But at no point in your discussion should you be talking about your products or services directly. At no point are you discussing your features and benefits. Instead, what you're doing is creating the question in their mind so that they will ask you the question, so they will come to you, and then you can start talking about products and services."

In the end, JLL and a good number of businesses we're learning about in this book are taking a practical approach to selling by defining influence differently. They're not pinning hopes on understanding customers "social graphs." Neither are they yearning to target ads better by cracking the code of friendships. Social media isn't about a better way to advertise. That's a trap. For these businesses, it's all about "planning the purchase": provoking customers to act in ways that ultimately lead toward purchase.

Marketers as Behavioral Architects

When we begin to see influence as behavioral, we appreciate the importance of *process*. Adjusting and improving the way social media marketing actually works cannot be done without improvements in process. But don't fear the p-word! Hang in there with me because what we're about to learn is super practical. It's a simple model for understanding what your customers want so you can figure out how to guide them toward your products.

So what does this model look like? Well, it doesn't look much like advertising or public relations, where we continually *remind* customers to buy. There's less focus on "reach-and-frequency" of message delivery, for instance. This updated, interactive process is more like shepherding. Think of it as guiding customers as they move from awareness of a product to consideration, then selection, then repurchase and advocacy. Marketing messages are certainly used along the way, but they're not the focal point.

"The focus is persuading visitors to take action," says best-selling author Bryan Eisenberg, who calls this model *persuasion architecture*. It's a concept and term many successful businesses have adopted. In Eisenberg's words, persuasion architecture is defined as the organization of the buying and selling processes married to the information flow.

Eisenberg, who is founding chairman of the Web Analytics Association (www.webanalyticsassociation.org), says an easy way to grasp persuasion architecture is to compare it to something familiar. For instance, information architecture. Businesses design organizational systems to help people find and manage information more successfully. Similarly, successful social media marketing *persuades* your customers to take action. Eisenberg reminds us of the classic AIDA model: awareness, interest, desire, and action.

"It's one of the oldest and most durable cognitive models (describing buying and selling process maps) because it helps marketers appeal to consumers' emotional and social needs," says Eisenberg.

> *Creating awareness, interest, desire,*
> *and action is still the game.*
> *Social media gives us a chance to focus*
> *on the "Action" part!*

He insists the AIDA model does not get tossed aside as part of a radical technology-driven revolution. Rather, this is our big chance to focus on the A part—action. That makes the AIDA model an *invaluable* source of guidance when designing practical social processes that sell.

Given today's more empowered, hyper-connected, advertisement-adverse customers, we certainly need a reliable way to sell online, a way that recognizes how prospective customers are not all at the same stage in the purchase process.

For instance, some customers are ready to make an immediate decision, others are still doing research, and others may be at various "in-between" stages. Persuasion architecture helps us be successful in addressing the needs of each kind of prospect and not merely in ways that influence them, but in ways that serve their needs.

In essence, persuasion architecture is based on Eisenberg's idea that everybody on the planet does things for their own reasons. These reasons translate into four distinct preferences or "ways of deciding." These are the "how" and "why" people do the things that they do. Eisenberg says that once you understand the four basic personality types, you can build "snapshots." These perspectives give you insight into *how* groups of your customers shop for your products—or "the how and why" that drives their purchase behavior. For most businesses, these are emotional, logical, fast-paced, and disciplined buyers.

Eisenberg says once you understand the "how," then you can build the "who." You can design processes that cater to them, that guide them down the sales funnel. He calls these group personas. Think of them as buyer groups displaying specific behavioral characteristics. For instance, some customers make decisions based mostly on speed; they just need to get it done. Others make them very meticulously, having qualified the decision inside and out. You know, the "due diligence" types who need to cover all the bases. These are two very distinct behavioral shopper groups. Thus, how people buy can be translated to "who is buying."

It's easy to think of these personas as profiles—small pictures that give us a better understanding of who the customer is, what their typical behavior is. For instance, "David the Decision Maker" or "Gail Get-it-Done" were two personas created by Debbie Qaqish of Pedowitz Group in her outstanding blog, "How to Create Content to Generate Demand" (www.oth.me/debbieq).

Bryan Eisenberg is nothing short of a genius when it comes to distilling practical success principles and making them actionable. Make no mistake, his approach is more like interactive, behavioral shepherding of customers. His concept is designed to help customers guide themselves as they move from awareness to consideration to selection and repurchase. His books include *Call to Action: Secret Formulas to Improve Online Results* and *Waiting for Your Cat to Bark? Persuading Customers When They Ignore Marketing*, and they are essential reading. Eisenberg, who blogs at www.bryaneisenberg.com, strips it down to practical, easy to execute basics.

A Customer GPS

Practically speaking, I like to think of behavior-based influence as navigating customers through what branding expert Jonathan Salem Baskin calls their "chronology of purchase intent." Or said another way, marketing becomes a GPS system for customers. Rather than using a group of satellites, customers use a variety of informational tools to navigate toward a "best fit" for their needs. These tools fit into categories like social shopping, sharing, recommendation, educational and advisory, reviews and comparison shopping.

For instance, consider how customer reviews have taken hold, specifically how they've improved the *process* of buying and selling online. Providing "virtual shelf space" for customer-generated reviews has become an effective way to guide customers toward products and services. Review tools are a great "social" example of behavioral influence. They're tangible. We can "work with" or "sculpt process" with them. We can elicit, publish, and make use of reviews in ways that serve our immediate goals and those of our customers. For instance, we can allow shoppers to rate the helpfulness of other customers' opinions. In this way, we're helping them suit themselves better.

Indeed, when customers give feedback that we literally see, it motivates behavior. Whether they're delighted or disgruntled, this feedback guides behavior of other customers. Independent research from Chicago-based E-tailing Group confirms review feedback is useful in optimizing more and more satisfactory shopping behavior. Of course, customer reviews are but one example of how social sellers are leveraging behavior to help customers guide themselves toward their wares.

The businesses we're meeting in this book are using various behavioral tools to help customers navigate their own evolving "chronology of purchase intent." No, they're not ignoring the traditional idea of influence, but they are positioning social media tools like global positioning satellites, helping customers navigate toward a best fit for specific needs.

Big Seed Marketing

"So where is this all going? It's hard to tell, but if I had to guess, I would say that we'll end up with an approach that looks a lot like the marketing tactics of the past," says Moxie Interactive's Greg Satell. "Despite the increasing sophistication of influence measurement, virality is still a crap shoot."

Satell goes on to point out that social networks like Facebook, Twitter, and LinkedIn are beginning to change the data infrastructure of the Web "by exposing connections that heretofore were hidden from marketers."

Satell concludes, "One thing is for sure: we are embarking on a new media paradigm where old truths are being infused with fresh possibilities."

But what does that mean, really? Satell points to academic researcher and now Principal Research Scientist at Yahoo!, Duncan Watts. Specifically, Watts has gone head-to-head with Malcolm Gladwell. His groundbreaking Columbia University paper, ***Influentials, Networks, and Public Opinion Formation 2007***, shows that while some of us are more influential than others, the likelihood of a single influential setting off a viral chain of events isn't much greater for anybody else. It seems Watts and experts like Rachel Happe agree. You can read the full paper at www.oth.me/wattspaper.

"Watts' solution? Mass media," says Satell, who warns those ignoring Watts do so at their own peril.

Watts' reasoning has been dubbed "Big Seed Marketing." Here's the rub. Because influence is so hard to track, it's much better to start with a lot of reach. Watts calls this the big seed. Then marketers use social media to amplify it.

"It seems to me to be an incredibly reasonable and sound approach," says Satell.

Are age-old ideas like Jack Trout's positioning and practices like public relations and advertising going away? Certainly not. But they are having less effect on demanding, always-on customers. The jury is out. Traditional forms of influence aren't enough these days. Neither are some of today's most sexy theories on networked influence very practical. Behavior is on the rise, and it's a vital piece to selling off the hook.

Reflection Questions:

1. Influence this! How does your business use Facebook, Twitter, or for that matter, search engines like Google and Yahoo? Are your efforts stopping at merely creating attention? Let's find out. Review your strategies for messages that lure customers toward taking actions. If you do find some, great. Now put them to a test. Do the actions help you discover and respond in some way to customer needs? For instance, are you storing customer information (a profile, insight on "need state," e-mail address, etc.) gleaned from the interaction? Are you directly responding to customers as a result? This will give you a good feel for how (or if) your business is putting influence to work.

2. Redefine. Are you putting influence to work in ways that create behavior? Consider how Jones Lang LaSalle is using YouTube to motivate executive decision makers into taking action—picking up the phone and starting "conversations worth having" with the company's account team. How might you use short, punchy videos or blog posts to inspire meaningful action among customers and prospects? Identify hot buttons that customers or constituents will be most disturbed, excited, frightened, or enticed by. Now apply them. Ask yourself, "What is it that we're seeing in the market (a risk, opportunity) that other people are not talking about right now? And how might that 'ah-ha' give a customer reason to view that insight in a compelling enough way to produce behavior" (i.e., an inbound lead)?

3. Persona very grata. Could your business put Bryan Eisenberg's idea of building personas to work in ways that push prospects from awareness, interest, and desire toward an eventual action? What are your customers' typical ways of making purchase decisions? Consider building three or four basic personality types, or snapshots. Brainstorm ways to leverage these insights into behavior. In other words, take what you've learned in other chapters and mix it with your new insights on "the how and why" that drive customers. "Architect" ways to interact with your customers that produce useful behaviors.

CHAPTER 6

PUTTING IT TO WORK

"Continuous effort—not strength or intelligence—
is the key to unlocking our potential."

Winston Churchill

S O what will it take for your business to continuously discover what's relevant, meaningful, and useful to customers? And how will you turn that knowledge into leads and sales? This chapter lays out next steps to meet the challenge. These are ...

1. *Get back to basics.*
   Set aside the technology and focus on solving customers' problems. Shut off anything that's noisier than it is useful. Follow customers, not gurus, catchy trends or "best practices."
2. *Plan everything you do; make each tactic connect to leads and sales.*
   Design behavioral processes that exploit classic direct response tactics.
3. *Translate customers' evolving need by publishing and serving.*
   Listen, then publish useful information that prompts questions that your products answer.

Have you ever wondered why we don't see books on "Telemarketing: An Hour a Day?" or "Direct Mail Marketing: An Hour a Day?" Sure, these things can be done in an hour per day, but not in a way that moves the needle. Social media marketing isn't any different. This chapter will show you how to make the most of your time, but we won't be discussing how to "do social media in *x* minutes per day." We'll discover how to make "the thing to be doing" the one that produces sales. Think about how empowering that will be!

Twitter, Facebook, LinkedIn, YouTube, Slideshare, Bebo, blogs, podcasts, and so on: yes, you're on the way to using these familiar tools in better ways, but only after we get priorities and *processes* in place first. We'll get around to selecting the most appropriate technologies to help us along once priorities are in place.

Throughout this chapter we'll return to familiar ideas: interactivity, utility, context, relevancy, purpose, service, and translation. We'll use them to decide how, when, and *if* to apply social media technologies to create sales. We'll build a reliable framework that ensures your success, and you'll meet more remarkable people who have mastered success principles discussed throughout this book. These folks are inspiring, living proof that prioritizing social media marketing in ways that produce sales *can* be done, practically speaking.

Tune Out the Noise, Choose What **Not** to Do

Much of your success will hinge on deciding what you (or your team) do *not* need to be doing every day. To accomplish this, you'll need to start shutting off anything noisier than it is useful.

"It's official. It's now impossible to keep up with the irrelevant data, false claims, illogical conclusions, and plain bad journalism associated with positive claims about social media," says Robert Bacal, CEO of Bacal and Associates (www.work911.com), best-selling author of *Giving the Business to Social Media Research*.

It's hard to not feel just like Bacal. The din of misinformation is a major hurdle for our businesses. We're constantly being told "do this, do that, but not like this, this way." Most of us have been quick to follow social media gurus, and figuring out what *not* to do seems unnatural.

"No single person could even locate most of the misinformation. It's just as impossible to explain why and how the numbers are wrongly interpreted. There are simply not enough hours in the day. The 'expert pool' is totally polluted, and now mainstream media, who depend on these social media experts, are reporting completely bogus and nutty things about social media success," says Bacal, who clearly feels the pain of business owners and corporate executives charged with social media marketing.

But if misguided advice is dominating the scene, could ignoring the noise actually be easy? For instance, let's assume *most* of what we're hearing and reading about social media won't serve our cause. If so, it will be easier to tune-out the noise. Heck, it might even feel good to shut off the hype-machine!

Where to start? Let's tune out the noise. When it comes to social media marketing, there are plenty of opportunities to *not* invest time in trivial nonsense.

Action item: Next time you see an overzealous list of facts about how awesomely huge, fast, or urgent the social Web is, consider asking yourself how *relevant* that fact is to the task at hand, selling. If there's very little (or nothing at all) *to do* with the information, simply tune it out.

Yes, Facebook is the size of a country. And? YouTube is the second largest search engine. And? Fifteen percent of bloggers spend 10 hours or more each week blogging. And? Twenty-five percent of search results for the world's top 20 largest brands are links to user-generated content. And? Twitter is adding 300,000 users a day. And?

If you can't readily do anything with the information, just tune it out. Is it anecdotally interesting? Okay. But how is it *relevant to your business*? Do you have time for enthusiastic or impressive anecdotes that don't help you do things that plug into sales? Does your marketing team?

Next time you see a top 10 to-do list for Twitter or Facebook or "the top 5 ways to use LinkedIn marketing," ask yourself, "Does this fit into the context of serving and selling to our customers?" And, if so, how?

Action item: Consider the credibility of the source. Decide if the source is a distraction or if it *should* earn your time, and if so, to what degree.

Does the person or entity providing statistics or issuing edicts have a horse in the race? Do they profit from your business throwing money at social media? You might want to tune it out. Consider how often the source provides *credible*, useful information. If they do occasionally, stay tuned. If they do not—or not often enough to earn your time—change the channel.

Bob Hoffman, CEO of Hoffman Lewis (www.hoffmanlewis.com) and author of "The Ad Contrarian" blog (www.adcontrarian.blogspot.com), half-jokingly comments on the intent of many social media experts and agencies.

"So why are we so enthusiastically supportive of the myth of The Thing That Will Change Everything? Simple. It's the Age of Hysteria. Keeping our clients in a state of anxiety is just plain good business."

It's good habit to consider the *intent* behind what you're reading or hearing. Because the intent behind tips, research, or advice weighs heavily into the credibility of the source.

Make it habit to ask yourself: "Does what I'm investing time in serve a purpose beyond creating a sense of enthusiasm or urgency? Does the author or publisher provide advice within the context of our need? If so, can we actually act on the advice?"

When consuming new information about social media, make it habit to ask yourself, "What am I to *do* with this new knowledge? Is this information actionable in ways that serve my business?" If not, tune it out.

Shut off anything that's noisier than it is useful. Follow your instincts and customers, not gurus.

Get Back to Basics

Once you've managed to make daily life less noisy and distracting, you can expand the idea a bit. If you're like most businesses, you'll benefit by just saying no to a handful of popular, *tactical* activities that serve questionable purposes and saying yes to getting back to basics.

Remember, although you'll be eliminating "to-dos," there will be plenty left to do! Don't fear the outcome of your new habit. Your Twitter tweets and blog posts may be less frequent, but trust that setting aside the tactics for a moment *will* give you *more* of what you want, not less.

Case in point: Adagio Tea (www.adagio.com) is one of the most innovative, successful online sellers of high-quality tea. The company's use of social media is exceptional because it set aside the tactics for a moment, long enough to put customers and process before gurus and tactics. They asked better questions and made sure social marketing connected to sales. Let's quickly discover how they did it.

When it comes to high-end teas, proper steep time is critical. Too much or too little time will result in bitter or less robust flavor, so if a tea drinker is to fully experience what Adagio sells, they've got to get the timing just right. That's what sophisticated tea drinkers need. It's what they expect, so Adagio offers new and existing customers a "tea timer" (www.adagio.com/pages/timer.html). The handy electronic timer is available free. Anyone can access it. Once downloaded, the small application sits on your computer desktop, ready for use at any time. When having your morning or afternoon tea, just double-click and open-up Adagio's little countdown timer. Click on the kind of tea you're steeping on the list of your favorite teas. Then click "go." The countdown timer starts. The tea timer is even customized based on the user's preferences.

Adagio's strategy focuses on the idea of being extremely useful. In fact, it integrates its free tool with the daily lives of customers and prospects—tea connoisseurs. In doing so, Adagio qualitatively improves customers' experience with tea, which the company sells, of course. But Adagio's approach also improves its ability to find, court, and retain customers. The tea timer isn't just handy for customers; it's helping Adagio build a larger customer base and increase sales transactions.

You see, in return for this handy tool, customers and prospects provide Adagio with explicit details about tea consumption habits. Users also provide their e-mail address. Before the timer can be downloaded, users must quickly register and set preferences. This requirement serves two purposes: to customize the experience for the user, but also to provide information about the user's tea consumption preferences to Adagio. This process design allows Adagio to follow up with new prospects who aren't yet buying their teas and to tailor that follow up based on what the user is currently drinking (preferring). The tea timer serves to build a super-qualified lead list.

The company's use of social media is exceptional because it is so basic. Adagio *set aside the tactics* for a moment and designed. It put together a process first, a rather simple one that focused on the customer, not the tool and not the trend of creating applications for the sake of creating applications. Adagio makes sure its use of social media has processes that connect to sales.

Audit Your Social Marketing

Improving marketing processes is the key to selling off the hook. Companies like Adagio are living proof. Making social marketing serve your businesses better means better design of social marketing itself. That's why your business will benefit from calling a time-out on some (or all) tactics to assess your process savvy. Here's the goal: eliminate time-wasters and identify better processes to develop and refine.

Most likely you or your marketing team are spending significant time blogging, tweeting on Twitter, posting updates on Facebook, or sending e-mail newsletters to customers. The tactical necessities of e-marketing are keeping you busy. All good. Leaders like Adagio are busy doing these things, too, some better than others, and that's entirely the point.

Are each of the tactics you're investing in today really necessary? Are some more worthy than others based on the outcomes they're generating? Most likely, there are tasks that you or your business invest time in that should be eliminated, freeing up time to design better processes. Just about every business can benefit from a quick social marketing audit.

"One of the most important aspects of decision making is understanding the choices you make," says Moxie Interactive's Greg Satell. "Examining your own thinking will not only improve your results, it will allow you to learn from your inevitable mistakes."

Most businesses will benefit by blowing a whistle, stopping to catch their breath. This gives us the ability to identify which tactics should be eliminated and which can be improved, all with creating better, more practical processes in mind. For instance, Malcolm Gladwell's "Law of the Few" (wherein a few influential people power massive change) is exciting and promising. But can such theories or mathematically complex social graphs be adopted by businesses who need practical answers today? Experts like Greg Satell think so.

"Social networks are an increasingly active area of serious academic research," says Satell. "We can expect greater insights to be uncovered in coming years."

But for now, remember the Golden Rule. Any influence you create must produce outcomes. It must ultimately connect to sales. As advertising legend David Ogilvy said, "We sell—or else!"

Remember, behavior is your secret weapon. Take full advantage of social media's ability to cause it.

Action item: As a first step, create a simple ranking system. The idea is to quickly and easily score each Web marketing tactic you're currently engaging in. Tactics that don't reliably produce sales and leads will rise to the top by using a simple, graphical approach.

Start by creating a four-column table with the labels Tool, Outputs, Weekly Hours, and Outcome Score (see diagram). Fill in row headers with your tactics, things like Twitter, Facebook, product reviews, LinkedIn, and so on—anything you're investing time in today.

Now simply identify your outputs—what each tactic is producing. Write them inside the appropriate box. Your outputs will include things like Web site traffic, sales leads, newsletter subscribers, followers, and friends. Next, log the total weekly hours being invested in each tactic. Finally, give each of your Tools an Outcome Score. Be brutally honest, and if you run this exercise through a committee, average the scores given to each tool in your final chart. Once you have identified the Outcome Score of each tactic, you're ready to make decisions. Be decisive. Be ruthless. Do you have tactics scoring two or less? Consider putting them on hold or eliminating the tactics entirely.

Greg Satell offers practical advice. He says to avoid consistency for consistency's sake. "It's natural to feel committed after making a decision, even a bad one. Yet there is no reason to double down on a bad bet. If it is within your power to make a decision, it is also within your power to change it."

Action item: Reassign the "recovered time" of your resource (you, your employee or agency's time). Designate that time to *design processes*.

Tool	Outputs	Weekly hours	Outcome score
Twitter	Followers, retweeters, Web site traffic	2	2
Facebook	Friends, engagement, occasional Web site traffic, newsletter subscribers	4	3
E-mail newsletter	Web site traffic, sales leads	8	4
Product reviews on site	Customer recommendations, product feedback, sales	6	4
RSS feed	Web site traffic (search engines)	6	4
LinkedIn	Followers, Group subscribers, Discussions, likes	4	1

Overall, a social media audit will help your business put its best foot forward before you start executing tactics. It will give you a place to start, a means to start identifying and eliminating time wasters so you can quickly develop better ways of architecting customer behavior. For more on making that happen, stay tuned!

The Fallacy of Best Practices

We're all human, and that means we're programmed to choose the path of least resistance. But is cutting ideas that work for others and pasting them into our environment the best way to get results? Let's take a quick look at why chasing best practices is often a waste of valuable time and how discovering and applying knowledge of what doesn't work is often a more productive way to invest your time.

"Our brains, contrary to what most people think, have been designed to learn much more from lessons learned from what didn't work; from conflicts; from situations that were everything but successful; from what would force us to rethink what we've just done and do it better, trying harder next time around," says Luis Suarez, an IBM knowledge management consultant.

Suarez is a prolific blogger (www.elsua.net) who points out that if enough of us are practicing a "best practice," it's probably on its way to becoming a rather mediocre, common practice and that we should always be leaving room to improve existing knowledge by acquiring more. That seems obvious. But the DNA, if you will, of a best practice isn't structured that way.

You see, the concepts supporting the idea of a best practice suggest static, fixed, unbeatable, *perfect ways of doing things.* Yet those characteristics are not what learning is all about. Acquiring knowledge is dynamic, flexible, modifiable, flowing—a continuous experience. The very nature of improving through learning is *imperfect.*

The whole idea of a best practice implies an absolute—that there is something better than everything else out there. But how many sure things are there in life? Suarez prefers to use the term **good practice.** As he says, "There is always room for improvement. Always! And that's exactly where best practices fail to deliver time and time again."

Chasing sure things isn't just unrealistic. Practically speaking, it's not effective. Best practices don't really work because what works for others probably won't work for you. Think about the idea in context of your personal life. If you've ever read a self-help book you know the truth: What works for others doesn't always work in *your* specific situation! But what **will** work for you is failing—discovering ideas that do not work and applying what you learn from the experience.

You may find the value being eked out of a given best practice is meager and hard fought, and not just because you weren't first, but because you're not architecting and improving the practice based on the specific needs of your business environment. By copying, you may be avoiding the learning process, and that's a critical part of the success formula.

Resist fearing the *imperfect nature of learning.* Instead, gain confidence by learning what **doesn't** work and making adjustments to improve results. It's a better way to invest your time. Can you still try **borrowing** practices that work for others? Sure, but be ready to fail sometimes.

Action item: Are others' best practices helping improve your business? What's your track record? Consider how many practices you've applied and failed with. Have most of them been tried before by other businesses? More importantly, the idea may be able to work in your business environment with some refinement. Apply what you learned in failing to your advantage when trying again.

The Purpose of Case Studies

Let's be clear. There are very successful companies selling access to huge libraries of case studies. They often call some of the strategies within them best practices, and that's fine. I even recommend that you subscribe to a few and buy their reports. But the good people at companies like eConsultancy (www .econsultancy.com), MEC Labs (www.marketingsherpa.com, www.market ingexperiments.com), and MarketingProfs (www.marketingprofs.com) will tell you the same. If a case study seems useful, the way to apply it is up to you. Selection and application of "learnings" you extract from a case depends on your intended purpose, competitive landscape, target market, and various other market contexts.

Bottom line: I'm using short stories and case studies in this book so you can make use of them. Tips and examples within them relate to various kinds of business environments, but it's up to *you* to decide which tips and examples actually "relate enough" to your situation. I'm equipping you to make better deci- sions. But you must ask, "Should the practice be applied to our challenges—our specific business context? How? Why?" Books and case studies provide guide rails, but they're not shortcuts.

"There are companies that are considered legends of customer service and held up as examples of how to treat customers. Zappos and Nordstroms come to mind as the most commonly mentioned. It's true that these companies are good exemplars of how you can build a company around customer service, but here's the problem: if you try to copy them, you will fail. Pure and simple," says customer service expert Robert Bacal of Bacal and Associates.

"These companies are singular companies. That is, they exemplify what works with *one* company, with a very specific culture, in a specific industry, and often the success of these companies is because of the people who drove the companies to be extremely customer service–oriented. You don't have those people. You don't have the culture or any of the variables that you will need to effectively model your business on theirs."

"It's like saying we should all copy Einstein, only none of us have Einstein's brain, or education, or experience. There was only one Einstein. There will never be another one, just like there will never be another Zappos. To try to be Einstein or Zappos is to fail."

Bacal says, "Build customer service strategies by looking at your business, its values, and those of specific customers. You can still build a company that succeeds in business, and you can do that in your own way that takes into account the specifics of *your* business, not Zappos."

Sure, it's common, understandable, and heck, it's human nature to seek silver bullets. But it's foolish to look for one right answer that's better than all the rest. Seeking out best practices won't serve your business very well because the means to understand what's right for *your* business involves discovery and iterative improvement. Learning. No shortcuts.

"I have been blogging for about seven years now, and plenty of folks have suggested I put together some of those best practices on blogging," says IBM's Luis Suarez. "Kind of like a *'Blogging 101' for newcomers*. And time and time again I keep telling those folks that, yes, I could do that. I could document them. But I also mention that they would only probably work for me and *my context*. No one else's."

So it's critical to define your company's translation process on your own—to learn, iterate, and improve. That's why successful businesses are *borrowing* effective processes from case studies and the remarkable companies providing them. They're applying the "good ideas" of others within their specific context to create sales, and so can you.

Action item: How is your business approaching case studies? Do you use them for entrepreneurial brainstorming and inspiration, or are they being applied to improve marketing processes and outcomes? Explore how your business is using case studies and best practices within them. Determine if case studies are used as guide rails and idea starters or shortcuts to success. Look for projects where case studies are being used successfully in ways that incorporate your business context to improve sales.

Making the Most of Your Time

Have you ever met someone who is remarkably calm, confident, and successful when it comes to business? Someone who instinctively knows what to do, how, and when—all without spinning wheels and wasting precious time? These successful people aren't afraid to fail, and that's part of their success. "Just doing it" has advantages, but when selecting and applying social media strategies *that sell*, there's another critical part to achieving success: avoiding what will not work. In other words, not wasting time.

> *Ryan Safady always knows what social strategy will work.*
> *But he doesn't have superpowers.*
> *He observes customers—lets them make the decision.*

Ryan Safady is one of those people who always seems to know what will work. But in reality, he doesn't have superpowers. His secret is simple: he follows customers and observes what they're already doing in social spaces. As a result, he draws conclusions about what customers might be willing to do with his company and what they're clearly *not* interested in doing. Once he's observed customers and drawn conclusions, he makes a decision. In doing so, he is saying no to certain strategies without even realizing it and investing time in what he knows *will* work. By letting customers guide his decisions, he's able to quickly decide which social media strategy to apply inside two very different kinds of businesses. Safady is making it look easy to sell off the hook.

But it's easy to get hooked on the idea that gaining customers' attention and engaging them is enough. There are plenty of "pushers" peddling the notion that occupying customers' time in social media will earn sales. In fact, many of today's most popular business gurus encourage us to do what we're familiar with. Grab customers' attention, but over here now on Twitter, Facebook, and so on. But grabbing at customers' attention is not enough. It has never been enough. Relative to what you could be doing with social media, it is a big waste of time.

Remember Abraham Maslow and his Law of the Instrument? Give someone a hammer, and everything starts looking like a nail. If you think about it, we marketers are on a mission, but if the only tool we have is engagement, social media starts looking like another nail. It feels a lot like advertising, and that's why most businesses are "just doing" social media.

Facebook, Twitter, LinkedIn, Google+, and whatever comes next are just nails to be hammered down in a world that already has too many nails.

Your business is probably broadcasting Twitter tweets, "blasting" e-mail, uploading YouTube videos, or posting blog entries, and there's nothing wrong with that. Most businesses do these things in hopes of attracting customers, and many times they succeed. But how often is the engagement that is generated wasted? You're investing time, energy, and money in creating attention, but are you any closer to capturing sales? You may hope to be, but are you *really*?

Don't worry. You are not alone. Despite all the blogging and tweeting and friending, leads and sales remain elusive to most businesses. They feel like they're wasting time because they are. Social engagement that consistently leads to sales requires something more, and Ryan Safady understands exactly what's needed—that is, a better way to invest time in social media, one you can feel confident about.

When Safady isn't renting Lamborghini cars and Boeing business jets to everyday people looking for a thrill, he's selling fabric to do-it-yourself crafters. By day, he rents luxury cars, yachts, homes and planes at his company, Imagine Lifestyles (www.imaginelifestyles.com). By night, he's selling novelty fabrics at his family's New Jersey-based fabric store (www.jandofabrics.com).

Both of Safady's vastly different businesses are using different approaches to social selling, and they're thriving. Imagine Lifestyles is rapidly expanding on its way to becoming the country's premier luxury rental business. At J and O Fabrics, a business started nearly fifty years ago by his grandparents, year-over-year sales, new visitors, and returning visitors are all increasing, all because of Safady's ability to apply social media marketing successfully in very different contexts.

Let Customer Behavior Guide Decisions

Safady's time is precious and limited. He's in charge of marketing for two *dramatically* different businesses, each with very different kinds of customers, and he's challenged to pick the right strategy for each. For instance, J and O Fabrics customers are chatty, very sociable, active (compulsive) buyers. They're vibrant, community-oriented people who are eager to join in—learn from, share tips with, and teach other arts-and-crafts enthusiasts. Imagine Lifestyles customers are far less chatty and not interested in being part of a community. They like finding new ways to celebrate life's successes through extraordinary experiences. J and O Fabrics customers are mostly female, hobby-oriented people who crave practical tips and love entering contests and learning new skills. Imagine Lifestyles customers are mostly male, working professionals. They're interested in the latest and greatest in luxury lifestyles, gadgets, cars, and the emotional rush that the fruits of success provide.

Safady is finding ways to make social media create sales in both situations. He's taking success principles discussed throughout this book and applying them, but he's doing so selectively, in two very different scenarios. He's creating sales in both companies by letting *observable customer behavior* guide his decisions.

For instance, given the nature and typical behavior of J and O Fabrics's customers, Safady is putting Facebook and blogging on the front burner. Arts and crafts hobbyists have been selling and building formal, informal, and ad-hoc digital communities for many years now. They're a very savvy group of digital natives. They're very active on Facebook and Web sites like Etsy.com, so Safady's use of Facebook and blogging focuses on *being useful, solving problems* for these customers. This decision just makes sense, practically speaking. It's what he and his team of two-and-a-half (one part-timer) focus on.

Answer Questions, Solve Problems

J and O Fabrics publishes blogs (www.jandofabrics.com/newsletters) and facilitates Facebook interactions (www.facebook.com/JandOFabrics) in ways that solve customers' problems because it's what they want. Tips and tricks are what they demonstrate a clear need for. That's their itch, so the company scratches it. Solving problems for customers is a means for Safady to lead them toward sales, not just engage them keep them occupied.

"More and more people, myself included, are trying to find answers to simple questions using search engines," says Safady as he describes his J and O Fabrics strategy. "It might be 'how do I resew a pocket to carry my keys, or how do I upholster the back seat of my '57 Chevy?' The more we blog answers to questions people are asking, the more we get discovered, and the more we have a chance to begin courting a new customer."

The lures Safady uses to create profitable customer behavior are equally practical. He's always mixing tips, tricks, and how-to blog features with compelling calls to action. He occasionally asks for the sale or prompts a registration. After all, his goal is to establish and nurture meaningful, ongoing relationships with new prospects—people who will eventually buy. And he's coaxing existing customers into buying more often, too.

Build Niche Knowledge Assets

Once Safady started seeing results from his question-and-answer, problem-solving approach, he set the obvious goal: to own the largest database collection of sewing tips in the world. And he's well on his way. J and O Fabrics is building a niche knowledge asset that is designed to pay short- and long-term dividends. It's a sensible, practical objective considering the company's customer demographic and what they're *already doing* online.

Safady's content marketing team is constantly discovering and blogging about what everyday crafters want to know—innovations and solutions to problems that matter to them. Whether through e-mail, telephone, or mail, J and O Fabrics is listening for what matters and feeding blog readers (and search engine searchers) a constant, fresh stream of relevant knowledge. It just makes sense.

"For instance, we began to take a lot of calls and in-store inquiries on 'what's the best fabric to use for isle runners at weddings,'" says Safady. "It was an obvious blog topic that, today, still delivers consistent sales results for us."

Sure, Safady and his helpers are keeping it fun, too. Once he understood what strategies to employ and put processes in place, the company could get creative. This lean-and-mean team is inventing characters like Netfah, the popular "answer woman" of the regular Ask Netfah column. Want to make a fifties-style poodle skirt but without using felt fabric? Netfah can help. Or maybe you're a manufacturer of custom banquet seating who needs to find fabric that's flame resistant (not just retardant) or a way to make existing fabric flame resistant. Netfah is there to help. Need to understand what food-safe fabric you should use for your child's reusable sandwich bags? If Netfah can't help, Go Green Gina can. She's helping everyday people make their homes and sewing rooms greener, happier, and healthier, all because it's what Safady's market demonstrates a clear need for—what they want, need, and are willing to consume.

Action item: What are your customers *doing* in social spaces, why, and how? What are they demonstrating a clear need for? What itch can you scratch for them? What questions do they ask that you can answer in the form of a blog story, for instance? Consider prioritizing those questions asked most often, or focus on lesser-known tips or often-overlooked tricks.

Action item: How can you quickly pull together the beginnings of a content marketing asset (i.e., a blog, e-book, white paper, or video) that solves customers' problems? For instance, do you already provide tips and tricks to customers? Are you already helping them put fires out or do more with less? How? Where? Brainstorm a practical way to collect and organize this information using simple, accessible tools like a blog. Focus on providing practical information first. Then mix in creative ways to present the information like creating characters like Go Green Gina or blogging controversial opinions.

Action item: Heed the advice of Anne Handley and C. C. Chapman, authors of *Content Rules*, when they say, "Unlike journalism, your content strategy should begin with the *why*." They suggest asking yourself:

- *Why* are you creating the content you're creating?
- *Who* is your audience? Who are you?
- *What* do you want the content to achieve?
- *When and how* are you going to develop the content?
- *Where* are you going to publish?

Observe and Align: Add Value to Customer Behavior

J and O Fabrics has always focused in-store marketing on holidays, seasons, and events. Naturally, the business communicates these promotions online. This traditional, in-store practice offered explosive opportunity when owner, Ryan Safady noticed how his customers were *behaving* on Facebook. His customer demographic cannot stop sharing their craft-related photos on Facebook during various seasons and events. Suddenly, he saw another opportunity to align J and O Fabrics' promotions with what customers were already doing.

In other words, finding ways to exploit *the existing behavior patterns* of customers made a lot of sense. Setting aside questions like "do we focus on Facebook, Twitter, blogging, or videos?" made Safady's decision an easy one. In effect, it eliminated a lot of other strategies that *might* make sense. Based on *observable behavior*, this option made solid sense.

J and O Fabrics began blogging on event-driven topics like the "Top 5 Funniest NFL Fabric Crafts" during football season not to make people laugh, and not because events have always been a good way to create and capture sales. The company chose these topics because they connected with behavior. Customers and prospects were *already sharing* outrageously clever, crafting-related stories and photos in social spaces.

> *Safady's strategy is as brilliant at it is simple.*
> *He aligns traditional promotions in ways that exploit*
> *what he observes people already doing on Facebook.*

This observation presents an opportunity for J and O Fabrics to prompt more, similar behavior among prospects *in ways that occasionally connect to products*.

The company also runs an annual "Most Amazing Hand-Crafted Halloween Costume" contest. Here, Facebook fans and blog readers are prompted to register for the promotion by "liking" the business. J and O Fabrics gives-away a $50 American Express gift card to the most creative customer and 10 percent–off coupons for everyone entering. Uploading photos and voting is accomplished within Facebook. This part is key as it focuses on how customers routinely use Facebook to show off their creations to friends and family. As a result, others join the contest, "like" J and O Fabrics, and purchase fabric from the company. They're recreating costumes based on photos they've discovered in Facebook.

Safady's strategy is as brilliant at it is simple. He aligns traditional promotions in ways that exploit what he observes people *already doing* on Facebook.

Similarly, Rachel Farris of PetRelocation.com also keys on photo and story telling habits of prospective customers—pet owners who use Facebook. They simply cannot get enough of seeing happy pets, and that includes animals recently, successfully relocated by PetRelocation.com's team. Farris says it's not uncommon for a prospect to be told, "You're moving to Malaysia? We just moved a dog to Kuala Lumpur; you can see him on our Facebook wall!"

Both companies are adding value to customers' *natural behavior* and reaping the benefits—selling off the hook.

Action item: Does your business focus on "life moments" (anniversaries, newly-weds, expectant motherhood, housewarming, etc.) of customers when executing marketing campaigns? How about seasons or holidays? Are customers demonstrating in-store or online social behaviors within these contexts? How can you tap into those behaviors and start using social media to add value for customers and increase purchase activity for your business? For instance, say your customers use materials (your products) to create finished works, products, or improvements. Can you leverage their behavior, post-purchase, to your (and customers') advantage? Try to think beyond contests that involve voting. Get creative.

Another example: an oriental rug retailer might take notice of customers increasingly choosing their hand-woven rugs over carpeting for health reasons. Let's pretend that during the purchase process older patrons are constantly expressing concern over their childrens' choices—first time home-buyers, usually with (or planning for) kids. In-store sales staff at our make believe store are taking notice of increasingly concerned grandparents as "carpet toxicity" becomes a serious health issue. The store owner realizes this as an opportunity to nurture their customers' children, helping them learn about and choose good-looking, healthy, and durable floor coverings. At the point of purchase, cashiers are instructed to offer customers a chance do someone a favor. Transacting customers are prompted to help friends or relatives earn a free floor covering consultation or a percent-off coupon. All the customer need do is sign up the friend for the store's Healthy Home newsletter, which may feature a "Healthy Floor Covering" column, home décor tips for budget conscious families, local discount coupons on retail partners, and such.

By prompting customers in-store as they check out, the rug retailer targets qualified leads. It focuses on "life stage" moments—a new home purchase or an upcoming relocation. For example, each customer might be asked, "Thanks for your purchase today. Do you happen to know anyone who's recently relocated or planning on buying a new home soon?" Just as J and O Fabrics takes advantage of customers' urge to show off their creations, a rug retailer could exploit a customer's desire to help a needy friend or family member who's relocating, netting the retailer a lead. All in exchange for useful information provided to customers.

Action item: If you're a service provider, do your customers demonstrate predictable behaviors around events or during seasons or "life moments" that present you with similar opportunities? How can you help customers overcome a challenge, make a decision, save money, plan for the future, or enjoy the emotional end-benefit of your service in ways that encourage social sharing?

For example, a provider of wedding planning services may observe that before, during, and after engagements, most clients display the same behavior. Newlywed brides and their families are always seeking advice on first-time home buying, home decorating, insurance, and personal finance. They're busy planning for non wedding things before, during, and after the wedding.

So what's more important to brides and their families than finding answers to questions on personal finance or ways to "de-stress" just prior to the big day? If a wedding planner were to regularly publish tips and tricks on these topics it would create opportunities for brides and their families to *share them within their social networks*. For a wedding planner that spells opportunity to be discovered, appreciated, and differentiated in the minds of future prospective customers *and those within their social network*. Publishing valued, useful, and *relevant* advice is a great way to generate leads for a service business.

How can you help customers overcome a challenge, save money, or make a big decision? Brainstorm a way to help customers. Design the distribution of advice in ways that encourages customers to share their satisfaction or new knowledge with their network.

Prioritize: Eliminate the Possibilities

Ryan Safady's other company, Imagine Lifestyles, is tricky. This business focuses on providing a service: renting luxury experiences. It's a radically different beast, offering a serious challenge. Imagine Lifestyles's customers are displaying less overt behavior in social spaces as compared to J and O Fabrics. These customers are far less chatty and not interested in being part of a community. Neither are they looking for helpful tips or tricks, but Safady is making modest strides in selling to them using social media.

What's his trick? Again, this entrepreneur looks at customer behavior and eliminates possibilities. For instance, Facebook and Twitter are simply not a smart place to focus his efforts. His target market isn't flocking around these realms. They're not behaving as J and O Fabrics' customers are. Could that change? Sure, and he's keeping his thumb on customers' pulse as he learns more about their social media habits. Imagine Lifestyles participates in Facebook and Twitter, but the company isn't focusing on them with good reason.

Safady takes notice of how this business has a vastly different customer than does J and O Fabrics. The mostly male, working-class customers like finding new ways to celebrate life's successes. Often, that means enjoying extraordinary experiences, the finer things in life. For the most part, his customer is into *buying* stuff, not hand-crafting it.

"Imagine Lifestyles has a few different kinds of clients," says Safady, whose three-year-old business services high net worth clients, hotel concierge staff, and everyday people who enjoy treating themselves like royalty every so often. The latter market segment is of particular interest to Safady, considering how many people fit into it.

His customers are fascinated by and attracted to the latest and greatest in luxury lifestyles, extravagant foods, gadgets, cars, and the emotional rush that the fruits of success provide, or so Safady believes.

"The truth is we're using blogging effectively. We're penetrating the search engine results and seeing leads roll in, but we're still trying to figure out precisely what kinds of stories and videos our target market truly wants to consume, come back for, and share with others," says Safady, who's been focusing on profiling the sensational, emotional aspects of luxury lifestyles for three years now on his blog www.imaginelifestyles.com/luxuryliving.

So far, so good. Based on Google Analytics reports, leads are increasing as Imagine Lifestyles's blog subscriber list grows, and that supports his decision to focus the company on blogging. It's working. Safady's team at this business is even leaner: a part-time Facebook and Twitter resource and a full-time blog editor who also handles regional rentals.

J and O Fabrics and Imagine Lifestyles are proof positive: it's entirely possible to be "one of those people" who seems to always know what works. You *can* be a Ryan Safady—a business owner or marketing manager who always seems to know what will make social media produce sales. The key is letting customers guide your decisions, observing what they're doing in social spaces, then drawing quick conclusions about what they might be willing to do with your company. By observing customers, it becomes possible to chart a course, set sail, and rest assured that your social media strategy will sell off the hook.

"You really need to be persistent," says Mike Moran, author of **Do it Wrong Quickly** and formerly Distinguished Engineer at IBM. "That's the major quality you need. It's not that you need knowledge. You don't need to be really smart. What you really need is to be persistent. You need to say, 'I'm going to try this, and if that doesn't work, I'm going to try this, and if that doesn't work, I'm going to try this' and not give up."

"It's okay if you do it wrong," says Moran. "Just do it wrong quickly because then you'll get the feedback you need to start doing it better."

Or as Greg Satell blogs at www.digitaltonto.com, make decisions, make mistakes. But most of all, "you have to make peace with the fact that having responsibility means that you have to make decisions, and that means some of your decisions will be wrong. Fortunately, it is rare that any one decision will determine your fate. A mistake can always be corrected. A good decision doesn't have to be perfect, it only needs to get the job done."

Action item: What possibilities can you eliminate? Grab your audit chart (from earlier in this chapter) and refer to it as a guide. Consider the strength of each strategy in terms of useful outputs it produces. Now consider how your customers are behaving in each social realm. Are they active in some more than others? Take what you're concluding and apply it. Prioritize. Make decisions boldly. Remember Mike Moran's words: "If you're not doing it quickly, you're doing it wrong." Your customer will eventually tell you which things are working and which things aren't.

The Measurement Game

Measurement is one of the biggest processes marketers invest time in. Yet it's also the most maligned, probably because there's so much hokus pokus involved! The process of measuring an advertisement's ultimate ability to cause sales has been labeled everything from witchcraft to a criminal racket by CEOs and CFOs. But measurement is also a source of wasted energy for many social marketers, especially social media measurement.

The process of determining if a social marketing campaign is working (or not) and how to improve its return is where massive confusion lies. What to measure, how, and when is also where a good deal of digital charlatanism happens. This realm is where endless debates on *if* and *how* return on investment *can* or *should* be measured take place, for instance.

But some of the most practical advice you'll hear on the subject comes from social media consultant Rachel Happe (www.thesocialorganization.com), who says, "Just because you can't calculate ROI *does not* absolve you of the responsibility to measure your performance and try to improve it."

So is measurement where your business has a lot to gain? It seems certain. Let's quickly understand where measuring fits into social selling, but we'll do so at a higher, strategic level without getting bogged down into endless debates and tech talk.

Jim Sterne, author of *Social Media Metrics: How to Measure and Optimize Your Marketing Investment* (www.oth.me/jimsterne), reminds us that a number is just a number. For instance, 4,231 views and mentions to a viral marketing campaign is a measurement. But when compared to your personal best, company expectations, or your competitors' efforts, that number becomes a metric. It becomes indicative of value, importance, or a change in results when it's understood in context.

"Without context, your measurements are meaningless. Without specific business goals, your metrics are meaningless," says Sterne, who's literally written the book on how to measure metrics as Key Performance Indicators (KPIs).

Robert Bacal of Bacal and Associates agrees. According to Bacal, "One of the issues about evaluating success has to do with 'what is good enough' and the consequences of drawing wrong conclusions. Another is that your metrics need to reflect your *business* goals as directly as possible."

"The more you lower your risk of bad conclusions, and the more directly you measure success in terms of business goals, the more expensive the whole thing gets until the cost of measuring exceeds your profits. So what (most) people do (with social media) is measure what's easy to measure rather than what is meaningful to measure," says Bacal.

For instance, consider how most businesses measure their involvement with Twitter—followers. Yet most of us readily admit the number is meaningless. Most of us realize that the number of followers is not a score. It's a statistic. It's like "minutes used on your phone plan" or "number of claimed dependents." Our own, personal experience with Twitter creates this perspective because with every additional person we follow, the average "attention value per followed person" decreases. We simply cannot keep up!

Businesses that sell off the hook know what's working, what isn't, and how to improve because they measure as many meaningful metrics as possible. These fall into three groups of KPIs:

1. Direct response (behavioral)
2. Attitudinal (how customers view or feel about a brand)
3. Attention and engagement (time)

Here's the important thing to remember when reading this book: these three groups of metrics are *combining* to help marketers sell more, more often, in social spaces. Exactly how they're combining is not fully understood and can vary greatly. Again, measurement has been a war zone where mass media and direct response practitioners have duked it out, but for our purposes, we'll focus on keeping this one idea foremost: social selling is not purely dependent on behavioral metrics. But behavioral KPIs do offer more *practical* use over attitudinal and engagement metrics. In other words, don't get wrapped up in understanding your customers' social graph or quantitative aspects of Facebook and Twitter (i.e., your friend count or "like" rate or followers).

Direct response strategies and supporting metrics *are* powerful tools that each company profiled in this book is proficient at. More often than not, direct response savvy is a point of competitive differentiation. So find ways to work with direct response metrics like cost per order (CPO), cost per sale, cost per lead, conversion to sale, "churn" or attrition rate, and so on—metrics that can be tied to business outcomes with a little elbow grease.

For instance, Intuit's mobile credit card processing product, GoPayment, uses practical direct response metrics to drive increased sales on its GoPayment .com site. The handy service offers any small business owner with a smartphone (like a Blackberry or iPhone) the ability to accept and process charge card payments right on the spot. The product is genuinely compelling and solves a real problem for on-the-go small business owners. But even more compelling are the short video testimonials the company uses on its site.

Intuit's Web site solicits video testimonials: success stories from a variety of happy customers. The GoPayment site then plays the testimonials and monitors conversion-to-sale ratios. Using a tool called Video Genie, Intuit automatically optimizes sales. The tool notices which videos cause the behavior Intuit is looking for (a sale) most often. Based on actual, ongoing conversion-to-sale, Video Genie decides which customer stories are more *relevant* to the largest group of potential buyers. GoPayment.com's Web site simply plays stories that are most effective at earning the sale.

"By presenting authentic testimonials that were relevant to prospects' shopping context, GoPayment.com saw a 30 percent increase in conversion-to-sale. Customers wanted to see the product in action and hear a recommendation from someone like them before making the purchase decision," says Laura Messerschmitt, Senior Marketing Manager at Intuit. The company uses the strategy to continually optimize—understand and respond to prospects' evolving shopping contexts—and to sell more products and services.

Successful social marketing demands a unique degree of insight and knowledge. Behavior on the Web can be measured, after all, and getting the most bang for your buck (optimizing) demands a constant process: develop, execute, measure, adjust, execute again, measure, and so on. But be careful to avoid wasting time in long-winded debates. Focus on behavior.

Plan: Make Gestures with Outcomes in Mind

What if each social media marketing tactic you engage in is actually a gesture? As Dictionary.com defines it, a gesture is an "action, courtesy, communication, etc., intended for effect or as a formality; considered expression."

For instance, when Anne Handley and C. C. Chapman discuss content marketing in their book, *Content Rules,* they're quick to point out how it must solve problems for customers.

"Your content shares a resource, solves a problem, helps your customers do their jobs better, improves their lives, or makes them smarter, wittier, better looking, taller, better-networked, cooler, more enlightened and with better backhands, tighter asses, and cuter kids. In short, it's of high value to your customers in whatever way resonates best with them," say Chapman and Handley.

Now think about gestures in the context of what we've learned so far. What are businesses doing when they're being "more useful" to their customers or working to be forever relevant, in context, and service-oriented? They're making gestures.

In prior chapters, we learned how powerful it can be when *everything* your business does (with social marketing) connects with sales. Now let's make it happen in your business by focusing on gestures.

Let's start with a quick example. Maybe you've been lucky enough to visit an ING Direct Cafe. The bank operates strategically-placed cafes, complete with low-cost, yet surprisingly good quality food and beverages. The "online only" bank even offers free Internet access, free financial market advice, and free meeting space to just about anyone who needs it. It's all part of the design.

These generous gestures seem disconnected from a bank, especially since the company's business model hinges entirely on having no physical branches. But in many ways, ING Direct cafés are actually helping prospects and customers save money from low-cost eats to meeting space and everything in between.

Similar to AnchorBank's Financial Answer Center, ING Direct is providing everyday people with better ways of getting things done, and these improvements are coming from an unusual helper: a bank. From meeting to eating, this bank is here to help. Sure, some gestures are just discounts or freebies, not really helping customers *invest* money. But that's where it gets interesting because in return for these acts, ING Direct earns the right to access customers and prospects more frequently and in intimate ways—ways that a pure Web-delivered experience cannot replicate.

Think about it. Customers and prospects hang out, conduct business, eat, drink, socialize, and maybe watch the latest financial news flash by on flat panel monitors, all on ING Direct's turf.

Design Gestures to Sell, not Brand

At first glance, this sounds like another branding gimmick. But it's not, considering the strategy's design. For instance, the ING Café in Chicago ran "Bike to Work Week" Specials. Every bicyclist that rode to the ING Direct Café during national Bike to Work Week was treated to a free bike valet, beverage, and tune up. As bikers participated, they were politely asked if they'd like to speak to a Café associate about "other simple ways to save your money." ING staffers struck up conversations that were *designed* to elicit information—knowledge on if (and when) bikers could find benefit in an ING Direct product.

"When people find themselves with available time and nothing available to do, they're open to receiving a pitch," says author and branding consultant Jonathan Salem Baskin. "Waiting in line. Sitting on a jet looking for its gate. TV channel-surfing. Creatively making those situations better lets you risk selling just about anything."

In this light, the bank isn't giving things away as a publicity stunt or to "brand themselves" as a caring corporate citizen. Neither are they just trying to occupy customers time in hopes they'll hang out and trip over a product on their own. ING Direct is spending *quality* time with customers—not looking to help them simply pass time. The *design* of gestures serves a purpose.

Contrast ING Direct's strategy with Patelco Credit Union's Bank on Trust campaign. Geared to foster trust for their brand that ultimately converts into new account holders, the credit union ran the "Patelco Pays Your Way" promotion. Patelco staffers surprised consumers by paying for their gas, groceries, coffee, and lunch by giving away $75 gift cards to supermarkets, coffee houses, and sandwich shops. In the end, Patelco spent $45,000 entertaining 1,500 San Francisco area residents. According to the bank's CEO, Patelco did it "to say 'thank you' to the communities and people who have supported us for the past 75 years since we could not have become the Bay Area's second largest credit union and number 5 in California without their support and continued trust in us."

But is entertainment an effective alternative to selling? "It's not, and it never was," says Jonathan Salem Baskin. "It's like thinking all you need for a great book is a lot of words and punctuation, or that a smiling face in a photo constitutes a happy moment in time. Purpose matters, as does how you accomplish something."

Baskin says customers know we're trying to sell to them something, and he asks an important question: is it possible that consumers suspect our motives when we make gestures without any admission of sales intent? Could the all-time lows in corporate reputation and credibility be partially a result of these acts?

"We can entertain or give away all we want, but perhaps we're just swapping empty social calories for the substance we once aspired to deliver," warns Baskin who is perfectly suited as co-author of, *Tell the Truth: Honesty is Your Most Powerful Marketing Tool*.

Both ING Direct and Patelco are making gestures at serious expense and with generating new accounts in mind. But only one is designing processes to make sure that actually happens. ING Direct is making investments in prospects, existing customers, and expensive real estate in an effort to sell, and the bank is upfront about it.

While some banks are making cosmetic changes to how branches look and feel and giving things away, innovative banks like ING Direct and Anchor-Bank are designing gestures and tracking their success. Unfortunately, most forward-thinking banks aren't talking much about their success with gestures. We're early-on in the game, but they are tracking progress. For example, they're measuring increases in accounts-per-household and products-per-household as compared to branches who have yet to implement such strategies. Similarly, "average deposit" and "average loan relationship" are also being studied when measuring the success of gesture-based programs.

Action item: Rethink the purpose of content—free knowledge you share with customers. This sage advice comes from content marketing expert and blogger Debbie Qaqish (www.oth.me/revmarketer) of Pedowitz Group, who says, "Content for the demand generation marketer is about *inviting* online behavior that shows where the prospect is in the buying cycle, then allowing an automatic or manual response."

Qaqish says gesture-oriented content marketing is all about an exchange of value that sets up the next behavior. So how can you start "chunking down" the content and reusing it as much as possible to create an insightful behavior? For instance, can you take a longer white paper and publish it in five parts and earn subscribers to the series? Consider designing the subscription to earn feedback on where your customer is in the buying cycle.

Reward New Customers with Success

Gesture-based marketing isn't limited to financial institutions, and it isn't limited to businesses taking initiative. Sometimes customers take control. Multi-channel retailer Tractor Supply Company (TSC) is well-known for making remarkable in-store gestures since 1938. And today the company is receiving them, too. According to Andrew Heltsley, TSC's marketing manager, backyard chicken clubs are using their parking lots and in-store spaces for meetings.

"All that does is funnel more business into the store because they're out there advocating for you," says Heltsley, who's excited at the chance to use digital media to leverage gestures.

"We're core to the lifestyle," says Heltsley. "As long as you're relevant to the core customer segment, they can't discuss the lifestyle without you. Because we helped them *get into* the lifestyle, we help *support* that lifestyle. When customers need a meeting space, they come to us."

Ex-urbanites and a fast-growing number of city dwellers are an important customer segment for this retailer. Witness hugely successful sites like www .backyardchickens.com and www.communitychickens.com. In response to increasing interest in raising "backyard chickens," TSC made a gesture. It developed a successful, education-focused content partnership with *The Chicken Whisperer*. TSC also partnered with Purina to create a "chick registry" (www .oth.me/chickreg). Customers who own chicks simply register them and begin to receive timely news, care tips, and coupons based on the age of the chick via e-mail. These helpful, new "digital gestures" come together with TSC's long-standing, traditional acts to *generate measurable demand* for products.

Like any business, keeping customers addicted to products is important, especially so for TSC. Heltsley says it's easy to think of chickens as the starter drug of livestock. But it's important to keep his comment in context because this retailer realizes that its most valuable customers are those who keep animals. So TSC is very interested in helping customers get started with animals as soon as possible and to the extent that they're terrifically successful at raising them right out of the gate.

Heltsley says if people decide to take the leap—to become a weekend farmer or more serious gardener—they *must* have support. New customers won't be able to buy products without the help, period.

"People need guidance to do things—and do things correctly—so that they're rewarded with success. There are going to be stumbling blocks along the way, and we'll be there for that, too. But the quickest way to build the relationship is for them to have some success because then they're going to try something else, and before you know it, they're buying everything in the store that supports the habit—if you keep with the drug analogy," Heltsley says with a grin.

That's why TSC is taking its offline, non-Web "gesture expertise" and leveraging it online. That's why Heltsley is eager to help customers get started with chickens using digital forms of education. He's gladly investing in helping new customers gain confidence and skills on raising chicks in the short term because doing so increases his ability to sell products in the long term. How does he know this? This is how TSC's customers have always behaved. The Web just gives Heltsley a new tool set.

Just the same, remember PetRelocation.com from chapter 1? Director of operations Rachel Farris says her account team does a great job of prompting customers to make *return* gestures. Just like eBay prompts happy buyers to rate their experience with sellers, PetRelocation.com's service specialists prompt customers to share a photo of their happily relocated pet on the company's Facebook page. In fact, most customers jump at the opportunity.

"They are usually very thankful for our help and as a result want to help us in return," says Farris, who says customers' gestures are often aimed at helping other pet owners. She says social media gives them the ability *to act on their empathy*. Customers feel for other pet owners who are experiencing the same stress, fear, and uncertainty they did when considering moving their pet, and they want to help others.

Bottom line: To be useful or relevant to customers, you've got to start *doing* things for them and allow them to do things for your other customers—all on your turf.

Action item: How can you commit your business, today, to helping customers make vital life-stage decisions or get important everyday things done? Consider ING Direct's Cafes, Tractor Supply Company, AnchorBank's Financial Answer Center, or Adagio's tea timer. Consider Adidas's Runbase Store in Tokyo, which offers showers, locker rooms, and weekly workshops and events. Brainstorm how you can start on any of these concepts on a smaller scale. How can you borrow from their design? Don't throw out ideas that seem disconnected from your product or service. Examine your list. Do any gestures increase your ability to make what you sell more relevant? Do any place your offering in better context? Any that *do* are fair game and can probably be designed to deliver measurable results.

Action item: Is your business *saying* things to customers with social media campaigns or *doing* things for them using gestures? Are your acts *designed* to produce behavior? Do they connect to a larger system or "selling process"— your sales funnel or customer life cycle? Think of each social marketing tool you employ today. Many of these programs may be generating customer behavior. If so, does each behavior prompt your business to follow up with another action? Is it part of a larger system you've designed?

Let's consider Adagio's initial gesture. Isn't it a bit of an ethical bribe of sorts? Tea drinkers get a free tool that's relevant (if not necessary) to their everyday lives. In return, customers are offering up qualitative information about themselves. But there's more. In response, Adagio makes sure the tea timer is preloaded (customized) to include teas that the user is actively drinking. Notice the multiple, predefined gestures from Adagio that add convenience and personalization.

Bottom line: Adagio is earning tea drinkers' participation by design, *through an exchange*—not a transfer of messages or ideas, but of behavior. It all starts with a gesture, and the company keeps following up with more gestures, each designed to earn more behavior so as to discover other needs, thus prompting more gestures. Of course, all of this give and take is aimed at ultimately generating a financial transaction and a thoroughly satisfying customer experience.

But what's new here, really? Consider your customer's chronology of purchase intent: awareness, consideration, preference, purchase, loyalty, advocacy. Notice that this classic marketing construct remains intact.

What's changing is your ability to discover momentary need states of customers along that time line and to put those discoveries to work for your business and customers. It's getting *easier!*

Do your social media gestures …	Yes	No
Give customers a chance to signal their purchase intent?		
Collect information on customers' purchase consideration stage?		
Solve problems or help customers understand them better?		
Help customers do something better, improve their lives or businesses?		
Allow your business to be more relevant to customers' context?		
Express admission of our intent to ultimately sell something?		
Connect with a lead/sales nurturing and/or direct response process?		
Get assigned to a person who analyzes responses and takes action?		
Take advantage of (incubate) newer, emerging markets?		
Leverage happy customers—give them incentive and a place to praise?		

Make Gestures Pay You: Respond to Response

Mortgage brokers and banks offer free new-home buyer workshops to inexperienced real estate buyers. They create quality time for prospects. Vacation timeshare companies have long used a similar approach, offering ethical bribes to fun-seeking vacationers. But what's the catch to the free vacation?

Again, quality time, and the marketer always asks for the sale—they get paid! Business-to-business companies have long used white papers and custom research, earning them leads and market position as "thought leaders."

Making gestures isn't a new idea. Gestures are premeditated, calculated acts that produce a measurable return: a customer response. But in the above examples, there's always *a response to customers'* responses built into the design, whether it's a hard sales pitch or a more nurturing response that eventually leads to asking for the sale.

Online social marketing gestures are the same. They can pay you, but only if you expect and design them to. You've got to be ready for customers' responses without fail, so expect and design gestures that earn *useful* responses, or don't make gestures at all!

Think back to the last time you were shopping online. Most of us have experienced a disconnected, isolated gesture, one that leaves you feeling abandoned. For instance, you've probably searched for a specific product using Google. Let's say you're shopping for a digital camera, a Canon A495. After querying Google, you notice an AdWords advertisement for a seller. The ad grabs your eye as the title reads "Canon A495—Free Shipping." You click it and are taken to a retailer's Web site, but now you're not viewing a product page of the camera, not even a category page for cameras. You're now viewing the front page of an e-commerce site featuring far more than cameras!

What just happened here? You expressed your intent to consider, or purchase, a specific camera via Google. You were told, "Come hither, I've got one and will give you a great deal, too," by an advertisement. But when you arrived at the Web site, the company paying for the ad told you, "I've got the camera, but now it's time to get to work digging through our Web site. Find it on your own!"

So what do you do? You hit the back button and start over again. Well, at least a good number of shoppers certainly do! Unfortunately, many businesses are inadvertently using pay-per-click search advertising to make isolated gestures—acts that fail to induce another response from the customer, and it happens in social media marketing, too.

If your business is going to make an investment in baiting customers with a compelling, tempting ethical bribe it only makes sense to expect a response. Be ready to respond with a premeditated, calculated gesture, one that's designed to produce—that's right—another response that moves your prospect forward.

Action item: Ask yourself, "Where is our business already making gestures that earn a response? Where are we doing a good job of following up on (bringing to sale) those responses?" This simple exercise will give you a starting point. Look around inside your business—no matter how big or small—for models that already work. Now take those models and replicate them using tools like blogs, YouTube, Facebook, and even e-mail.

Action item: Ask yourself, "What problems are customers experiencing that we can offer a clever, unorthodox, or novel solution to? Might this give us an excuse to talk about our product in creative ways that bring value to customers or give us a reason to stay in touch with customers in ways that allow us to prompt more behaviors?"

Action item: Can you improve an underperforming lead-generation program using a social media element? Consider, again, where your business is making gestures that earn a response from targets. Is the follow-up process effective? Do you respond well or at all? Why or why not? Can it be improved (can you bring prospects to closure faster, more often) using social media tools? Is there something about social media tools that might *better serve* your need or your target markets' needs? For instance, would a sequence of short, educational video clips or provocative blog posts be more convenient for (or appreciated by) customers versus the telemarketing or direct mail campaign you're using?

Always Be Selling

Sometimes responses to marketing gestures come in the form of unexpected, critical feedback, like when a customer responds in writing to an e-mail message you sent out. But marketing staff may not see such criticism as an *opportunity* to translate customers' evolving needs—to ultimately help up-sell, cross-sell the customer. Often, the customer's response is forwarded to the customer service team for follow-up. But in fairness to marketing folks, most businesses don't have a clearly defined translation *process* for Web marketers to adhere to. As a result, marketing staff don't "go into sell mode" when presented with critical feedback.

Consider your Web marketing resource—whether it's just you or dozens of helpers. Do you expect customer responses after delivering a campaign message? Of course, we all tend to expect a result from marketing efforts. But what happens when unexpected responses are received?

For instance, let's say a software company's digital marketing team sends out a new product announcement. The company is encouraging a trial of a new software tool, but the marketing team isn't prepared for a direct, e-mail response from customers, and that's exactly what happens. Messages pour in. The replies are completely unrelated to the promotion within the e-mail blast that just went out. Most are angry at the company's recent decision to stop supporting an unrelated product line, a line whose customers are strategically vital to the company's near-term financial health.

In most situations, the responses will get passed to customer service. Let them put out the raging fire! Responses may completely miss the product development team. You know, the strategic-minded folks who are actively trying to avoid alienating thousands of customers!

Unfortunately, when most businesses get this kind of feedback, they "circle the wagons" and put out fires. They're not thinking about angry customers as offering *constructive* feedback. They're trying to solve a problem. They're not thinking to themselves, "Hey, this is a chance to find out what this customer's needs look like." But as we'll learn in pages ahead, candid feedback sometimes signals a whale of an opportunity and this requires responding to the customer's angry response, not just passing it to customer service.

Action item: How does your team view customer responses that criticize the company's decisions? Does your business have a means to respond to emotional customers in ways that *capture* useful information on their changing needs? Consider practical ways to create a process—one that captures this information and prioritizes it for future action.

Conduct a Symphony of Gestures

It's easy to see how a lightweight digital application like Adagio's tea timer can be used to foster mutually useful gestures. But what if we could take all digital marketing tools and design them similarly? Could we fashion e-mail, social media, product reviews, and affiliate programs all to guide customers down the sales funnel? What if we could make them *all* deliver and elicit behavior together simultaneously?

For instance, let's consider the *practical* view on Amazon.com's success. Everything Amazon's marketing team does elicits a gesture or directly prompts one. Ultimately, those gestures result in more sales. Of course, Amazon has serious database technology powering its success. But what makes that technology so special?

For instance, think about your own experience with Amazon: how you interact with Amazon and how the company interacts with you. Your gestures can be transactional (a purchase) or behavioral (a "softer" act). But if you think about it they always tend to lead you forward toward purchase, consideration, or repurchase. For instance, Amazon may witness specific kinds of customer behavior, like when you review or recommend a book, or it may explicitly gain insight on a specific need you have. Either way, the company takes note and files your gesture away for later use.

A Sales-focused Social Gesture Timeline

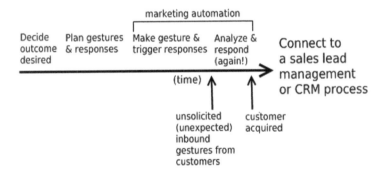

It's all part of a predefined, database-driven, direct-response process; one that gently, politely, but *deliberately* leads you. Amazon operates a system of gestures that uses e-mail, pop-ups, wish lists, last-minute impulse suggestions at checkout and mobile applications. For example, Amazon continually prompts buyers to "wish list" items or to rate a particular book reviewer's work for helpfulness in making your decision. Amazon's system may decide to e-mail monetary or non-monetary (e.g., free shipping) incentives to customers. The system constantly encourages customers to act in ways that create value for Amazon, including, but not limited to, purchasing.

Can this kind of multifaceted approach happen without the whiz-bang, super-scaleable technology that Amazon pioneered? Of course not. Do you need to run out and invest in similar technology? Not necessarily.

Action item: Take note of the *fundamental design* that Amazon's technology executes on. Borrow from it. Apply it within your business to drive similar customer behavior patterns. Use tools you already have easy access to. Start small, test, and adapt. Create your own profit-focused symphony of gestures using common tools like e-mail.

Action item: Where's your diamond? Where inside your organization are there places to tap into direct response expertise? Review resumes, strike up discussions in lunchrooms, use social networking tools like LinkedIn—do whatever you can to discover and contact employees who have hidden talents. Formulate ways to take action by tapping into them.

Action item: Ask yourself, "In servicing our customers, are there ways to feed back data about their behavior in ways that add value to them and move them toward our products and services?" For instance, consider product recommendations. How can we make such a simple idea come alive without over-complicating the technology challenges?

Translate: Compete on Service, Not Price

Is your business competing by selling at lower prices and higher profit margins? That's a tough assignment. What if you mixed in "diagnosing and solving customer problems" as a way to earn more sales, to differentiate? And what if you grew long-term sales by translating customers' evolving needs to boot?

Imagine educating customers. I'm sure you can envision something like that. But what if you could literally certify them as more qualified to do whatever they do better? What if you did it in ways that created demand for products and services? For instance, let's say you're selling to other businesses. Envision helping customers improve the outcomes your products produce—for themselves or their customers. Whomever you're selling to, if you were to provide buyers more educational value, might they discover new reasons to do business with you? Would they buy more often? Could being an actual teacher *differentiate* you from customers' other choices, like your competitors?

For instance, let's say you sell hardware supplies or tools. Imagine teaching customers how to improve their homes, literally certifying home-improvement enthusiasts as bonafide fixer-uppers. Your curriculum teaches passionate buyers everything from how to redesign their kitchen using the latest design software tools, to helping kids build safe, sturdy tree houses. Consider your own business and how powerful it would be to define what your customers should learn, at what pace, and why. Imagine how close you would get to buyers, especially if they were hungry to get better at what they need to do.

For instance, pretend you sell sales force automation software to other businesses. In this case, you're teaching customers all the ins and outs of how to organize, motivate, and run an effective sales team. Your curriculum includes teaching customers how to set good sales staff incentives and how to foster healthy levels of internal competitiveness among sales people or structuring an effective sales retreat. Even if you're selling products like hand-knotted oriental rugs or mobile device replacement batteries, think about the educational aspects of your product, and think about it in ongoing terms. Do clients need continued advice, or could they benefit from continuous informational interactions?

Action item: Think in terms of your business. What are the little-known facts or tips and tricks—bits of information that you may take for granted but customers find empowering? Write them down. Ask yourself, "What are the three biggest obstacles preventing our customers from selling more to their customers? How can we be helping them address these challenges in ways that are easy for us (and them) to execute on?" Write down your ideas. Now hold your ideas up against the first list of little-known facts, tips, and tricks. Invent practical ways to bring your educational ideas to life in ways that share useful tips and tricks.

Recall HubSpot's Grader.com suite of tools and Tractor Supply Company's educational approach to selling. These businesses are not disguising advertising as education. They aren't creating more sales by changing their image or manipulating customers' perceptions. Rather, they're making an operational shift, one that helps them play better offense, one that helps them sell off the hook.

Action item: Ask yourself, "If I were to teach customers tricks of the trade, would it give us an opportunity to generate more leads or sales? How could we start doing this tomorrow with a small-scale pilot program designed with sales in mind?"

Publish, Analyze, Respond—Profit

As we've discussed throughout this book, the idea of surrounding commercial pitches with useful, credible information or services isn't new. Consider infomercials. From Susan Powter's "Stop the Insanity" to Ron Popeil's plethora of informative pitches to the booming voice of Billy Mays, infomercials are proof that content sells.

Okay, print marketing fans. Consider the "magalog" (magazine plus catalog) business model. This direct marketing idea was pioneered by the likes of Lands' End and Drs. Foster and Smith. Publishing-based marketing practices are neither revolutionary nor out of reach for any company, and digital media offer significant cost efficiencies.

But setting up a blog does not make one a successful publisher, and trust isn't manufactured by default. As BrandBuilder Marketing's Olivier Blanchard says, "Publishing propaganda or marketing content is just that, regardless of the platform. Just because you publish marketing content on a blog doesn't mean it magically morphs into something 'authentic' that engages customers and will spread through word of mouth."

Successful online content marketing challenges us to borrow what works from proven, often non-digital, models that can sell off the hook. Then it's a matter of applying digital marketing tools in ways that supercharge results. Once again, the path forward involves leveraging what we already know works and *then* picking the right tech tools.

For instance, digital direct response pioneer (and long time cataloger) Crutchfield has been handing out trusted, useful information and educating customers for decades, and now they're leveraging traditional know-how on the social Web.

Crutchfield is a category leader in high-end audio equipment. Even in a slowing economy, they're not giving way on price. They've never been the low-cost leader in home and automotive sound systems. They're a higher-priced leader known for over-servicing highly sophisticated enthusiasts. Customers are serious audiophiles, demanding the best gear *and* customized solutions, and Crutchfield has earned its trusted brand based on the experience it delivers.

This product-based company has historically made big investments in high-touch services to customers. It's been accessing and making use of insights on customers' needs for decades. Crutchfield educates customers in ways they perceive to be free. For instance, the company's telephone-based customer service reps are deeply versed in electronics, audio components, peripherals, components, system architecture, you name it. They're highly trained *educators* that customers (who pay a premium on products) expect extreme levels of guidance from.

In effect, listening to customers is not a new idea to Crutchfield, and neither is educating them. That's why Crutchfield is publishing a how-to oriented, information-rich magazine. The company distributes it digitally and through direct mail. It's a full-blown online and print magazine (www.oth.me/audiomag). But make no mistake, this is a very practical "next step" in its traditional, educational approach because using digital media gives Crutchfield yet another chance to actively harvest, database, analyze, and act on behavioral cues. It's simply using a new channel to gain insights on changing needs, perceptions, and satisfaction of customers. The company is translating: publishing, analyzing and responding—applying knowledge gained to sell off the hook.

There's no selling going on within the magazine's pages. Instead, Crutchfield rigorously analyzes. On the digital side, the company studies "consumption patterns" of the knowledge it shares, and that reveals a variety of useful customer behaviors. Crutchfield studies how, when, and where customers are reading. The company then correlates that behavior to sales and customer satisfaction over a given period of time.

For instance, Crutchfield wants to justify its investment in content marketing. By observing how groups of customers behave, measurement becomes a practical tool to do that. For instance, the company is asking itself simple questions like, "Can frequency-of-purchase be increased among automotive audio system customers through consumption of related magazine content?

Can we take customers buying once per year and increase their purchase rate using educational content?"

Crutchfield is initiating a gesture through its new educational magazine, and then it's analyzing customer responses. They're doing so within the context of business metrics, outputs like purchase frequency and average order. Their marketing team is discovering if the magazine is working or not within various buyer or prospect groups. If it's not working, Crutchfield's team learns and reacts on-the-fly.

Crutchfield is optimizing. They're discovering the best customer groups to send magazines to—online and offline—"the best" being defined as those who ultimately purchase or purchase more often. Once customer groups that respond better are identified, the company turns-up the volume. It can direct more content aimed at similar customer groups.

Crutchfield is taking a knowledge-based model that already works and supercharging it by applying new tools. The company is giving information-hungry customers relevant, useful, educational information, and it's using digital distribution and real-time analysis to amp up the results. Crutchfield isn't reinventing the wheel. Their underlying business model is a proven one: direct, database-driven marketing.

As it turns out, the idea of competing by diagnosing and solving customer problems is not new. Neither is translating customer need using publishing a revolutionary concept. Yes, going "from zero to Crutchfield" could be challenging, depending on a company's level of experience and available resources. But executing on this core idea is not out of reach for any business.

Businesses like Adagio and Crutchfield simply ask themselves, "What do our customers and prospects need to get the most out of what we sell?" Adagio's customers need a simple countdown timer to make sure tea is steeped correctly. Everything Crutchfield's customers do needs to be on the cutting edge of audio gear. They demand continuous, qualified guidance and *practical information* that helps them experience music in new, exciting ways. Asking the question leads to obvious, actionable answers.

Action item: Is there a similar tool you might offer? What can you give customers to help them get the most out of what they enjoy in ways that connect with goods and services you're selling? How can the tool you offer allow you to use behavior as a secret weapon?

Action item: Ask yourself, "Where do most of our customers leave money on the table when using our product or service? What one or two simple things could they do differently that would multiply their return on investment? How could we help make that happen for them in ways that increase demand for our products and services?" Brainstorm ideas on how you can experiment tomorrow on a limited scale. Rank your ideas based on potential payoff and ease of implementation. Be realistic, and use your gut instinct.

Hooking Your Customers

Rok Hrastnik of infomercial company, Studio Moderna (www.studio-moderna.com) had a tough job. He needed to sell mattresses and bedding goods—items that customers don't need very frequently—online. To make matters worse, he'd have little help from his colleagues in the direct TV division. His team operated Web sites capturing sales from TV-generated attention. But he was given orders to create *new* customers using nothing but the Web.

Like most of us, Hrastnik was following. Most of his strategies were what everyone else seemed to be doing. For instance, he was using expensive pay-per-click advertising on Google and sending out e-mail newsletters that customers loathed. Nobody wanted to read about his bedding- and sleep-related products, and his pay-per-click search ads weren't working very well, either.

One day Hrastnik got creative and took a risk. He was already publishing a newsletter, but he decided to take a different approach. His plan was to stick with publishing but mix in Studio Moderna's in-house, gesture-based direct marketing expertise. His plan was to leverage what he already knew worked!

In a nutshell, his plan would ...

- Establish meaningful relationships with *unqualified* customers who would eventually buy
- Grow those relationships exponentially (organically) by giving readers incentives to recruit others

- Offer his unqualified prospects honest, durable value—useful knowledge that they actually wanted
- Net sales—be there with a compelling call to action when his prospects became ready to consider a purchase
- Prove a profit—spend less on producing and distributing content than he would get back in gross sales

Like most marketers, one of Hrastnik's many challenges was that mattress sell-cycles are long. *Really* long. People don't buy mattresses very frequently, and buying leads of qualified bedding seekers was far too expensive. So he decided to amass as many nonqualified buyers as possible. He would create a list of prospects relatively cheaply and keep them busy consuming high-quality content.

	Qualified Customers	Un-Qualified Customers
List size	10,000	100,000
Cost per e-mail	1	0.15
Total cost	$10,000	$15,000
Conversion rate	10.00%	2.50%
Customers acquired	1,000	2,500
Cost per order	10	6
Revenue	$100,000	$250,000

Hrastnik set to work trying to figure out what lure he would use to attract and successfully hook his prospects. What was it that *unqualified* customers would crave or truly need—enough to keep reading his newsletters? After racking his brain for a while, it came to him like a bolt of lightning.

As marketers, we're in no position to judge what's right or wrong for customers in terms of what they want. Does it really matter what "it" is that customers need or find helpful? Need is need, and that was Hrastnik's big revelation. Between the anticipated point of purchase and today, he would give customers what it was that they needed, *whatever it was*. He would cater to that need in a way that produced value. He would scratch any itch customers came up with!

First, Hrastnik acquired a large, unqualified, permission-based list of e-mail addresses. He mailed a vacation sweepstakes offer to recipients. This built his prospecting list. As part of his promotion, subscribers agreed to receive newsletters full of information on what they really, truly wanted and could use to improve their lives immediately.

E-mail isn't new. Publishing isn't new. Neither is the idea of an ethical bribe that keeps customers engaged long enough to make a sales pitch. Again, consider vacation timeshare marketing strategies. Hrastnik was familiar with these ideas. In fact, direct-response TV (informercial) companies like his are masters at information-laden sales pitches. Good content is the bait that hooks customers. As a result, they stick around long enough to hear the pitch.

Segmented by gender, his newsletters included topical content focused on issues appealing widely to men and women. Women were treated to successful courtship, beauty, and weight-loss tips. Celebrity gossip also resonated with women. Men received well-written, boldly designed newsletters on grooming tips, gadget articles, automotive, and sports content—the kind of stuff that men typically consume, appreciate, and share.

Just to spur readers' behavior a bit, Hrastnik kicked it up a notch. He allowed subscribers to increase their chances of winning the sweepstakes by making referrals. If a subscriber referred a friend (to join in the contest, thus becoming a subscriber to his list), their chance of winning a prize increased.

To Hrastnik's glee, most contest applicants stayed on. They *liked* the newsletters and agreed to receive occasional promotions from Dormeo.com, Studio Moderna's mattress and bedding brand. In fact, subscribers liked the newsletters so much they passed them on to friends, growing the prospect list organically. Of course, they demonstrated a clear level of tolerance, unsubscribing when receiving calls to action (promotions) too frequently. Hrastnik noticed that *three* promotions per month was optimal. Readers were demanding respect.

Dormeo.com Email and E-commerce Data
(total email clicks/site views and sales transactions)

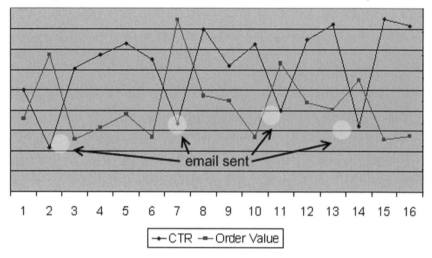

But his bet was on target. Hrastnik was able to keep prospects around and engaged long enough to make occasional calls to action, to create awareness and purchase consideration. And, yes, they even began purchasing mattresses. As seen in this chart, customers slowed down consumption of Dormeo's content when they were transacting. That's when the brand was sending out calls to action and promotional email messages. Logically, when customers were not receiving promotions and transacting, they were reading e-mail and Web site content more often.

In the end, Hrastnik established meaningful relationships with *unqualified* customers, enough of whom eventually purchased his products—enough of his product to make a significant investment (in content) profitable. Dormeo's costs were offset by sales. Sweepstakes and content production costs were kept low enough to make his cost-per-order (CPO) look good on a spreadsheet.

Hooking customers on content and reeling them in over time works. It's a practical way to sell off the hook. Businesses like Studio Moderna are living proof.

Action item: Ask yourself, "How could we execute on Dormeo's five-step plan? What do our customers like to do in their downtime? And how could we play a role in ways they perceive as valuable *and* give us opportunities to make calls to action?" In the case of a business-to-business or service company, you may also want to ask, "Can we use this blueprint to design a marketing program that gains insight on customers' evolving needs?"

Hooking Customers on Your Service

Imagine Lifestyles (mentioned earlier in this chapter) approaches blogging just as practically as Rok Hrastnik approaches email-based content marketing. Owner Ryan Safady's goal is to become the leading luxury news and information destination on the Web. His strategy is simple: attract prospects, earn a continuing relationship with them (via e-mail), and nurture subscribers (leads) to fruition—convert them into renters of luxury experiences. He succeeds by providing stories and videos his target market wants, appreciates, enjoys, and actively shares. He peppers luxury news and information with occasional, *authentic views of first-time luxury rental experiences in a way that ...*

- Plants a seed (the thought of renting a luxury experience); and
- Keeps subscribers reading and sharing his newsletter and blog.

Often focusing on the sensational, his blog is an original source of celebrity news (like luxury auto thefts and wrecks), eco-friendly luxury, upscale dining tips, exotic cuisine, and "the most expensive things." His short, punchy features focus on luxurious places, foods, people, cars—the over-the-top lifestyle experiences themselves. Through storytelling, the company highlights lots and lots of the "finer things."

But Safady is careful to also weave in a surprising fact every so often: These kinds of experiences are more accessible than readers think. The company often pairs this suggestion with presentation of the *"emotional* end benefit" of a first-time luxury experience. It's a subtle hook. Safady plants seeds in prospects' minds by proving and dramatizing just how *accessible and exciting* renting a luxury experience can be.

So far, the company is blogging but also spending more time on video testimonials. The treatment is straightforward, no fancy gimmicks, scripts, or special effects. Safady documents customers' dramatic reactions though real-life, first-time experiences. His approach is simple: let customers share their honest excitement and exhilaration. He believes capturing this kind of emotion and making it available to others is the best way to start everyday people *considering* the experience. Showing them an authentic view of a first-time luxury experience plants a seed that Safady nurtures with his blog.

For instance, one video lets viewers ride along with a customer named Eric as he learns how to drive a Lamborghini for the first time. Give it a look: www.oth.me/ridewitheric. You can feel Eric's excitement and honest nervousness as he begins his experience. You can almost sense what's coming next. Sure enough, Eric quickly gains confidence in how to "paddle shift" the car just before he punches the accelerator a bit on an open road.

Action item: Ask yourself, "What emotionally compelling stories can we be telling to attract and hook prospects over time? What kinds of stories does our target market want, appreciate, enjoy, and actively share? And how can we integrate subtle calls to action into stories that plant seeds in minds of customers?" Specifically, identify typical objections prospects give when considering your service. With this context in mind, brainstorm ways that you can literally prove those objections to be either false or based on preconceived assumptions. Think in terms of video testimonials or blogs, just like Safady does. Consider how, starting tomorrow, your business can initiate and guide customers' *behavior* using dialogue or stories they crave in ways that prime the pump for products and services.

Desire Lines: Let Customers Set the Context

Are there ways to let customers tell you how, when, and where you should be selling to them? Yes, indeed. Reviews inherently ask the question "what do you like" and "what do you not like?" about a given product or service. It's the negative that invites criticism. But sometimes this open invitation also results in *expression of creative use.*

For instance, think back to Vintage Tub and Bath in the prior chapter. The company invited criticism of a toilet seat and was given valuable insight:

customers were using the product in a creative context—gifting. Let's find out how your business can make an easy habit of letting customers show the way. Let's make the idea of discovering customers' "expressions of creative use" actionable so you can capture hidden sales.

Consider educational science equipment company Arbor Scientific (www .arborsci.com) as an example. Like most online sellers, the company is allowing customers to review products on its Web site. But the company's marketing team has little time to read product reviews, especially with finding hidden sales in mind. But they should, and so should you.

For instance, feedback on Arbor Scientific's e-commerce site shows grade school teachers (the company's primary target market) using their products in innovative, unforeseen ways. The company's light spectra/fragmentation glasses are typically used as teaching aids, but some customers are using them outside the classroom. As it turns out, teachers are spicing up wedding receptions using the glasses.

Suddenly, Arbor Scientific's product is becoming a high-impact, low-cost favor at wedding receptions. The glasses are mixing nicely with flashing lights and disco-balls on the dance floor and in ways that finally get Uncle Frank out on the floor! The context in which customers are buying this product is *shifting* in unexpected ways. Customers are using the glasses creatively.

Gunnar Branson calls these creative uses "desire lines." Originally described by Gaston Bachelard in his 1958 book, *The Poetics of Space*, a desire line is a path left by people's use of space. For instance, consider the erosion created in the ground as people and animals take short cuts—walk over vegetation toward their destination.

"Most parks and college campuses have desire lines etched in the grass lawns—areas where people took short cuts off the carefully designed, planned, and constructed concrete footpaths," says Branson. "Frustrated landscapers have long tried to keep people from destroying the grass and flowers by creating fences and other obstacles, but they rarely work. People tend to simply walk around those obstacles, creating new desire lines."

"Instead of fighting desire lines, it is possible to put them to use. Many designers will intentionally delay the building of walkways for several months and instead just plant grass around and between buildings. After a few months, the natural traffic of students will create desire lines in the grass that can be read as a plan for final concrete walkways. A wider path is built in the deeper areas of erosion and a smaller path in the light areas because the desire lines illustrate where more or less people walk," says Branson.

In Arbor Scientific's case, the space being etched is a customer review on a Web site product page. Desire lines can be found everywhere, not just on the ground.

"Whenever people move through their lives, interact with others, buy things, change things, and improvise or hack things, they leave a path. Sure, all people don't always follow precisely the same path. But the desire lines can be read and understood," says Branson.

For instance, social community expert Rachel Happ says, "People contact organizations on their blogs, Facebook pages, and Twitter because the existing mechanisms are too complex and have been so over-engineered that they are no longer humane."

So what if the desire lines of Arbor Scientific's customers were fed back to the company's product marketing organization? Can the company exploit a newly identified, potentially lucrative market—specifically, weddings? Think about it. The company could begin selling this product during spring time, normally a dead season for school supplies. Arbor Scientific could extend this product's selling season or even boost profit margin by catering to the wedding favor market.

Further exploration of this discovery could lead to the company setting up a low-cost, single-product microsite, a Web store catering to low-cost wedding favor shoppers. The single product store might be surrounded by useful tips and tricks on do-it-yourself, budget-conscious wedding planning or a blog.

Often times, hidden demand *is* making itself noticeable. But you've got to be looking for it.

Arbor would be wise to quickly identify if there is serious sales potential here in a new market. By using tools like Google, one can quickly study demand for low-cost wedding favors. Search engines allow us to observe demand for products and gain insight on how well that demand is being met by sellers. For instance, Google's advertising platform provides tools that show how competitive certain keyword search terms are and how many monthly searches are being conducted on certain phrases. We can also observe advertisements themselves and Web sites competing for searchers' attention.

Action item: Consider Vintage Tub and Bath from chapter 3. Ask yourself, "Do we have under-performing products or services that hold potential?" Examine product and service reviews for hints on how customers are using your products or how they're extracting value in ways you've not fully appreciated. Identify ways to remerchandise (or reshape) these products to match how you observe customers' shopping for them. Then reintroduce your products back into the market.

Action item: Ask yourself, "Is anyone at our business listening for customers' expressions of creative use—looking for desire lines being created by customers? What practical resources can we use to start monitoring, analyzing, and acting on what we learn? How can we put those resources to work in practical ways?" Be sure to focus on discovering easy (yet sometimes unorthodox) ways customers are using products and services. Act on discoveries in an organized way. Once you've found one, run it through a quick qualification process. Decide if it's worthy of action. Act on customers' shifting context. Match their desire lines in ways that sell off the hook.

Turn Negative Criticism into a Constructive Force

In the prior chapter, we discussed how innovators like Zappos succeed at discovering and cashing in on unmet demand. By now it should be obvious to you. Luck and happenstance aren't at work here. These companies are finding ways to tap into strong, hidden currents of demand for products. They are living proof: it *is* possible to discover what customers don't know they need and exploit the opportunity, but only if we're willing to see something negative as a positive.

Gunnar Branson says his clients are discovering and capturing unmet demand using social media as a secret weapon. He says the key is prompting customers to signal what they're *not* interested in.

Branson suggests, "Instead of asking customers and prospects what they need, give them opportunities to express what they *don't* need. People tend to be more specific when they are critical."

If you think about it, criticism is actually an optimistic and constructive act because to criticize requires an assumption that something better could exist. When people explain what they don't like about something, whether they realize it or not, they are silently explaining what they *do* want, what they really, *really* need.

Or, as Tom Peters once told Epsilon's employees, "Innovation comes not from market research or focus groups, but from pissed off people."

Branson asks us to think about it this way. What if a nineteenth-century focus group had asked people to talk about what they needed from a horse and carriage? Branson suggests, "We might have heard about the challenges of caring for a horse in order to travel. But what if we asked them to *complain* about personal transportation?"

Branson believes we would have heard about how expensive and unreliable horse and carriage transportation was and how burdensome it was to employ people to maintain the horse and carriage. In essence, the inconveniences were too great despite the grace, beauty, and power of a horse.

"Especially to those urban dwellers with less than a fortune or acres of land to spare," says Branson, who believes the early automobile manufacturers understood something vital.

There was less demand for a better horse and far more demand for private transportation, a way to get around that allowed urban dwellers to avoid horses altogether! In fact, more and more people were moving to cities every day. There was a fast-growing and *unmet* demand for personal transportation.

"The negative—trouble with horses—defined the positive—demand for private transportation," reveals Branson.

Action item: Think twice about prioritizing being liked in spaces like Facebook. Brainstorm ways you can start exploiting customer dislike tomorrow. How can you begin prompting customers to signal (or explicitly tell you) what they're *not* interested in using social tools? How can you apply that knowledge in ways that qualitatively improve customers' lives through better shopping experiences (e.g., Zappos) or products (e.g., Apple's iPods)?

Profit from Customer Dislikes

Consider Renée Mauborgne and W. Chan Kim's *Blue Ocean Strategy* (www
.oth.me/blueoceanstrat) approach to successful selling—that is, choosing not to
compete in a traditional sense. Mauborgne and Kim say today's most successful
companies are selling more by innovating, choosing to bypass competition with
other sharks in bloody, "red ocean" markets.

The new phenomenon these authors describe is founded in the constructive
force of negative criticism. Think about it. Companies like Hubspot, River Pools
and Spas, and PetRelocation.com are creating uncontested market space that's
ripe for growth rather than competing in existing markets. These businesses are
competing in leagues of their own.

These companies are not simply in the right place at the right time, with the
right product or service. They are capitalizing on *what customers do not like* about
existing products and services.

Many businesses we've met in this book are designing social experiences
that lead to sales—rising above grabbing at attention or engaging customers. But
they're also redefining the market by serving customers in previously unheard
of ways. For instance, there are many fiberglass pool companies in America, but
there are very few like River Pools and Spas.

In their book *Blue Ocean Strategy*, Mauborgne and Kim profile Callaway
Golf. This company discovered new demand for its golf clubs by asking itself
an interesting question. That is, why were noncustomers shying away from golf
itself? Rather than fighting to win a share of the golf market, Callaway asked
itself, "Why aren't people taking up golf? What don't they like about it?" It's the
kind of question Marcus Sheridan of River Pools and Spas asks himself all the
time.

As it turned out, Callaway found one commonality among a large group
of noncustomers: hitting the golf ball was perceived as being too difficult. As
a result, golf was not enough fun for novices, so they avoided golf altogether!
Callaway responded and successfully sold off the hook. They simply built a club
with a bigger head. They made it easier to hit the ball. The move opened up
a new market of novice buyers, and it even appealed to players in the existing
market who were having similar problems!

In the end, you can discover what people are complaining about by riding the New York City subway every morning and afternoon during rush hour, or you can use focus groups that, with some luck, ask the right questions, too. But social media tools offer a powerful, cost-effective means to discover and harness *negative* criticism to sell off the hook!

Action item: Consider prompting nonbuyers to express criticism about your products and services using social media. Make their responses actionable. Gather them up, analyze them, and act on the feedback. Nonbuyers are defined as people who know of your (and competitors') products and services but refuse to buy them. Don't worry about the tools you'll use to gather criticism. Just focus on what's easier for your business, more practical.

Action item: Ask yourself, "Why are all these prospects *not* buying what we or any of our competitors have to offer? Are there any *commonalities* between these nonbuyers?"

Other questions to ask yourself include ...

- "Do people choosing to not buy perceive products in a negative, frightening, or unappealing light? Why? How can we take advantage of these negative perceptions? How can we start addressing them through products themselves (innovations), merchandising, and compelling uses of social media?"
- "What legitimate fears, misinformed views, or popular (but false) myths are discouraging customers from buying our products or services? How can we address them in positive ways that provide value to customers *and* provoke them to take action?

Next Steps

This chapter demonstrates how your business can take the first steps toward selling off the hook. We've discussed three important next steps and presented ways to take immediate action on them. These are ...

- Get back to basics: Pick a few things to stop doing and focus more on solving customers' problems. Shut off anything that's noisier than it is useful to creating sales. Consider auditing how you're currently spending time and refocusing on what's really important. Reassign the "recovered time" to *designing behavioral processes that connect to sales.*

- Plan: Focus on addressing customers' typical questions and problems. Use preplanned gestures. Give customers answers that respectfully guide them toward products and services. Serve and publish. Avoid leading customers toward dead ends, and always provide a response to their response.

- Translate: Find the desire lines. Constantly listen to customers' evolving needs, and then act on them. Let customers decide what your ethical bribe—your bait—will be to get them hooked, whether it's a sweepstakes paired with lifestyle tips (Dormeo) or focused education (HubSpot).

You've now got the social process design tools to begin shaping behavior in ways that sell off the hook. Once you've put an interactive, direct-response–powered framework in place, you'll be ready to advance toward your goal. Evaluating and selecting appropriate tech tools to aid in your mission will be secondary. Whether it's YouTube, Facebook, Slideshare, Twitter, e-mail, blogging, or a combination of tools, remember how easy it is for Ryan Safady.

The gesture-based program you choose to experiment with first is your choice. Does one jump out at you as being most easily implemented given current resources? Maybe you'll provide useful video education to existing customers through more focused, purposeful blogging. You might blog to discover, qualify, and capture new customers using an "Ask the Expert" text-based blogging approach (www.oth.me/petexpert) like PetRelocation.com. Sure, you might choose to serve customers in relevant ways with innovative-but-simple digital applications. Then again, you might pilot an approach similar to Rok Hrastnik's—combining the lure of sweepstakes with desirable content distributed using e-mail and a Web site. You might even mix in Facebook.

No matter what gestures you choose, be sure to *design* them. Let them help you observe customers' behavior and translate need in ways that allow your business to forever be relevant. Do things that prompt questions from customers that lead toward answers—your products and services.

Communicating the Strategy

Strategy only works if it can be clearly explained to the people who will actually do the work of carrying it out, and I've done my best to make next steps clear and realistic. Ultimately, you're in the driver's seat. Maybe you're leading a team of one or a large group of employees or agencies. In either case, staying organized and on task will be critical to your business success.

That's why I've created a handful of free resources for my readers at www .makesocialsell.com/resources. Here, you'll find more useful tools for everyone from one-man (or -woman) bands to corporate or agency managers.

CHAPTER 7

I CAN SEE CLEARLY NOW

"When Kepler found his long-cherished belief did not agree with the most precise observation, he accepted the uncomfortable fact. He preferred the hard truth to his dearest illusions; that is the heart of science."

Dr. Carl Sagan

SADLY, most businesses dipping toes in social media waters are not experiencing a clearer, focused understanding of it. They're enthusiastic about tools like Facebook, but they're not seeing them in a useful, practical way, let alone reaping rewards. In fact, many experience affirmation of what they've come to expect from the shiny new tools. It's completely believable when social media yields so little!

"We are driven to increasing complexity, yet that is the very thing that gets in the way of the value over time," says social media consultant Rachel Happe, who sees many social tools evolving from simple novelties into bulky, complex messes.

But *observation* is power. Seeing is believing, and social media gives us that ability—to instantly, ubiquitously observe customers' behavior like never before. But are most of us observant participants, or are we just watching from the upper balcony?

In other words, are advances like Facebook and Twitter revealing a clearer path forward, or are they confusing us more?

Consider astronomer Galileo Galilei. Galileo made astounding observations with his improved technology, the telescope. With it, he proved Nicolaus Copernicus's planetary motion theory to be fact and Claudius Ptolemy's centuries-old fact to be fiction. Similar to Galileo's times, our businesses now have the ability to improve upon the tenets of a familiar-yet-outdated reality. I'm speaking of the limiting beliefs and practices born of the mass communications era. But something is getting in the way.

You may recall a scene in the Bill Murray movie *What About Bob*, where he's telling a joke. Murray says, "The doctor draws two circles and says, 'What do you see?' The patient says, 'Sex.' So, the doctor draws trees and says, 'What do you see?' The patient replies, 'Sex.' The doctor draws a car, an owl. 'Sex, sex, sex.' The doctor says to the patient, 'You are *obsessed* with sex.' And the patient replies, 'Well, you're the one drawing all the dirty pictures!'"

> *"The media and marketing industry ... has become blinded by metrics that it does not understand. Somehow, the notion of accountability has morphed into a misguided quest for the sure thing in the form of ROI metrics for just about everything."*

"The media and marketing industry has become blinded by metrics that it does not understand," says Moxie Interactive's Greg Satell, who sees the obsession with return on investment as one of the obstacles. "Somehow, the notion of accountability has morphed into a misguided quest for the sure thing in the form of ROI metrics for just about everything."

You see, for most of us, social media tools are *not* revealing a deeper, clearer reality. For instance, too few of us are learning how to sell more by serving customers better. Advances like Facebook, LinkedIn, and Bebo are confusing us more than they're making things clear, and that's where we see a break with Galileo's experience. His new observations made reality *clearer*. What we see and hear about social media are only making things seem *bigger and faster*—not clearer.

Yet the successes of companies like those we've met in earlier chapters compel us, urge us to reexamine our "marketing reality" and consider reshaping it into something that better serves our bottom line.

As we've discussed, the urge to make social media hit the bottom line is why measuring it has become such a priority. Indeed, if you don't measure something you cannot manage it. Smart business folks have understood that for a while now. But Jim Sterne, chairman of the Web Analytics Association and president of Target Marketing of Santa Barbara, makes an important point when he says, "Just because you measure social media doesn't mean you'll be successful at applying it."

Sterne underscores the role of purpose. He says having a specific goal for Facebook, Twitter or whatever tool you're using is essential. Otherwise you're just marketing for marketing's sake and measuring for measurement's sake. In other words, having an expected outcome for social media is powerful because it forces a business to measure in ways that produce meaningful outcomes.

"If you have a specific goal for Facebook then measurement can help you achieve that goal," says Sterne. "But if you do not have a focused goal then it's easy to end up measuring the wrong things. For instance, if you don't expect and plan ways for Facebook to produce leads and sales you're more likely to believe 'number of likes' is an inherently meaningful metric."

Sterne says metrics like 'likes,' clicks, and followers by themselves have no intrinsic value. But attaching specific goals to what we are now able to observe creates meaning. Observations become useful. What to do, how to do it, and why becomes clearer.

Of Torture and Obfuscation

Thanks to Galileo's observations, humanity reshaped its complete identity based on a radical shift in perspective. Instantly, our sense of reality changed based on what could be plainly seen, for the first time. Earth was not the center of our universe. Back then, this news was met with violent disagreement. After all, Galileo's new twist on reality was in opposition to over a century of mathematics-driven science—Claudius Ptolemy's science.

But Ptolemy's belief system was one relying on *partial* observation and incomplete math. Like today's mass media advertising industry, Ptolemy's system had been around a while. It was modified over and over so many times by so many scientists that it it became incomprehensible to the commoner. Hence, *knowing* that the Earth was the center of the universe asked you to *believe,* not observe. Sound familiar?

The similarities to today's mass media branding industry are striking. Consider how (outside of direct response) every print, broadcast, and digital ad is measured—proven to be real, effective. It's based mostly on incomplete observations and increasingly convoluted, tortured math. Mass advertising struggles to connect resulting behavior across multiple mediums. Consider also how many iterations of branding we've witnessed since the birth of advertising. A brief scan of history reveals Emotional Branding, Accidental Branding, Digital Branding, Nonprofit Branding, Iconic Branding, Luxury Branding, Faith Branding (for religious institutions), Branding Intelligence, and the latest, Personal Branding and Holistic Branding.

Like Ptolemy's system, marketing communications professionals are so confused themselves they cannot agree on a simple definition or a set of standards, whether it's measurement or the practice itself. It's gotten so crazy that veteran ad man Bob Hoffman cited a clever variation on that last one called Brand Holism in late 2009.

"Which I suspect is a branch of asshole-ism," quipped Hoffman, who rightly suggests that there is no way to satirize these overly complex, contrived "new versions" of advertising. They've become an illogical parody of themselves.

But humor aside, we can learn from this short story. Ptolemic science and modern day advertising share commonalities. Each is based on loose, fragmented observations that are easy to believe and almost impossible to see because each has been tortured by experts to the extent that what *was* once simple to understand *now* makes little sense. There are too many cooks in the kitchen!

If you think about it, making sense of advertising itself is a bit like predicting the motion of planets before the telescope: without actually observing them first hand. The math seems to work out in the end, but the truth is there's no way of really knowing. It's difficult, if not impossible, to *observe* what went right or wrong and understand why. There are too many variables.

As Albert Einstein said, "Any intelligent fool can make things bigger and more complex. It takes a touch of genius—and a lot of courage—to move in the opposite direction."

And that's precisely what Galileo's work did. It simplified and made things more understandable to humanity, more accessible because it was rooted in what people could *observe*, not what was easy to believe. Let's be clear: most of what Galileo saw, he wasn't inclined to believe himself! He simply could not escape his eyes.

In contrast to Galileo's experience peering through a better telescope, most of us dipping toes in budding, new social media waters are *not* experiencing a more clear, focused understanding. We're rarely seeing the market landscape in a more useful way, and we're seldom doing things in new ways. Again, we're experiencing *affirmation of what we expect*. It's no surprise when social media yields so little! But how have we gotten here? And can understanding our past oversights help lead us out of the weeds?

Pavlov, Advertising, and Social Media

Since social media's arrival, why has our modern-day experience with it been so shallow, hype-filled, and superficial? Why is it taking so long for most of us to exploit such a remarkable technological advance? We now know our businesses are not at the center of the universe; our customers are. So what's holding us back?

Advertising works, or so we've come to believe over time. One cannot argue with the billions spent annually on mass media advertising. And no matter how frustrated or disappointed we are with proving its effectiveness, we've never found a better answer to creating demand.

Aside from direct response marketers, most of us don't truly know if advertising is effective, how much so, and why. We've been *conditioned* to not need to know. We hope our ad campaigns generate profitable customers. Digital marketers *believe* they do based on likes, page views, impressions, opens, and other indicators of attention or popularity. Sometimes, chief executives are treated to incomprehensible explanations as to why ad campaigns are worth our time. In the end, we believe in advertising's effectiveness because we've always believed in it. We're conditioned to.

Have you ever experienced a marketing or ad campaign that's missed its mark by a long shot only to be strangely satisfied in the end? Most of us have. Maybe you exhibited at a trade show that should have generated 800 to 900 qualified leads but only netted 55. Or perhaps you made a huge broadcast or magazine ad buy that everyone predicted would have your phones ringing for 3 days, representing 5 figures of sales revenue—only to net $2,000. The result is almost always the same. Someone inside your company or at your ad agency ends up saying, "Although we missed our target, we got immeasurable branding value out of this investment."

This is a classic example of clashing expectations driven by *belief systems* that have become downright religious. On one side (the CEO, CFO, or direct response marketers) we have an expectation of clear, measurable return on investment. On the other, we have practices like branding—a strategy everyone defines differently and measures in mystical, intangible ways. Hence, true effectiveness remains elusive. Not knowing is baked into the practice. And so it goes with social media marketing. So far, most of us don't really know. It's why marketers continue to spend huge amounts of dollars on ineffective banner ads, for instance. We've been conditioned to.

Although it sounds crazy, a good number of business folks like it this way. It's comfortable because it's familiar, and that's just human nature. It makes sense when we fixate on measuring the quantitative aspects of social media. It's natural to pick the things that are easiest to measure and then rationalize their importance.

The truth is this: when it arrived on the scene, social media had no distinct marketing purpose. Neither did it have obvious, built-in measures. Being eager to adopt, we brought social media into the mix and applied what we know—advertising metrics and practices. So when measuring social media today, most of us apply a known standard: the way we measure traditional marketing communications.

For instance, practices like public relations are measured in quantitative terms. Results are measured in number of newspaper or magazine clippings, radio mentions, and impressions. These are things that measure success in a mass communications world. A viral Web campaign produces similar outcomes.

Is it any wonder that most of us have come to *expect* social media marketing to deliver so little? Should we be surprised when we believe ambiguous measurements like engagement are new when they're just a repackaged version of attention? In the end, we find ourselves hoping for the best—that social media delivers tangible benefits. But we *expect* the worst—that we'll never really know. We expect this out of habit and *accept* it. It's sufficient. The promise of social media marketing is merely following suit with mass advertising.

Now I'm not about to liken marketers to Pavolv's dog with all of this conditioning speak! And I'm not suggesting throwing the baby out with the bathwater. But I *am* recommending mixing in behavioral, observation-based marketing models (i.e., direct response) with practices that rely on partial observation and incomplete math (i.e., advertising), and I'm not alone.

In February of 2009, two advertising industry giants agreed. They said, "There is no longer a linear model of consumer behavior. The concept of AIDA (awareness, interest, desire, action) is now spaghetti. Direct response no longer exists at the end of the purchase funnel. Thanks to the digitization of everything, brand and response are now intertwined."

Remarkably, the two men were Daniel Morel, CEO of Wunderman, and John Gerzema, chief insights officer of Young and Rubicam Group (www.oth.me/brandandresponse). The heads of these massive global advertising agencies went on to proclaim that in a world of "compressed consumer decision-making, direct response is now a potent form of branding."

They went on to say, "To rebuild brand value, direct response can play a vital role. Brands are coming under attack because they're not fast enough in this new world. However, we have the tools, technology, data, and knowledge to learn, adapt, customize, and respond to stimulate not only sales, but contribute in building loyalty and affinity for the brand. "

The Rise of Digital Charlatans

The plain truths brought about by the World Wide Web have created quite a stir among mass marketing traditionalists. Just as Galileo experienced in the seventeenth century, the old guard advertising industry initially rejected the new truths revealed by the Web. For instance, the truth is customers have always had the power. The Web simply amplifies it, converting it to a deafening din. But today it's becoming increasingly evident: The whole of marketing communications is setting up for an exciting reboot. Even the purists are starting to accept today's new truths, but not without some drama.

Since the birth of Web marketing in the late nineties, mass media and broadcast-oriented advertising purists have feared what the Web might mean, perhaps because this new reality lets everyone participating (customers, marketers and middlemen) *observe and interact* like never before. Others suggest the Web's interactivity and transparency (on behavior) is the source of fear, that these ideas conflict with decades of mass media advertising ideas, dogma, and beliefs. Over the last decade or so, we've seen a classic art (creative) versus science (behavior) showdown setting up. But what does history teach us about avoiding pitfalls?

Consider what we have in common with astronomers like Galileo, Kepler, Copernicus, and Brahe. What these great men *saw* challenged their own personal, deeply entrenched, century-old beliefs. Quite suddenly, their observations were destroying what was held as proven science, facts born of greats like Claudius Ptolemy. Galileo (and his observation-based brethren) challenged the world's preconceived notions about planetary motion.

Well over a century after Ptolemy, Galileo finally toppled an incredibly strong, sometimes religiously driven belief system, but it took serious time.

Just as in Galileo's time, many businesses are still grappling with an updated, interactive, "always-on" reality, and for many reasons. For instance, consider charlatanism. Throughout human history, advances in knowledge and technology produce periods of adjustment. These transitional moments always give rise to opportunistic charlatans—people who exploit the excitement by declaring traditional knowledge dead. As a result, many of us enthusiastically join in, but we end up missing out because even in times of sudden change, fundamental truths tend to remain the same. Truths about, for instance, human behavior.

Sure, the way we execute against those truths change, but that's not nearly as sexy, exciting, and *distracting* as a "total revolution in everything." Hence, we end up chasing being "liked" or spending valuable time trying to answer questions like "what's a fan worth?" rather than "how can we make social media sell?"

The Web has forever made the world more connected and interactive. Communicating is no longer about "talking at." We can now "talk with" and observe. Even more exciting, the world of communications is infinitely measurable. But what has all the excitement led to so far? Well, most of us have learned one thing: the Web is a good broadcasting device. Blogging and micro-blogging (Twitter) have proven that fact, and that's why many marketers and agencies (and businesses that support them) are happy to be broadcasting on the Web, under-utilizing it.

For instance, consider our lexicon. Today, it's common practice to "blast" e-mails. Blast? Notice, we don't "target" e-mail or "send" it. We *blast* it. Experts like branding heretic Jonathan Salem Baskin say many of us use this language with good reason. The silly rhetoric of charlatans is in full control. We're following "expert" advice.

"I bet people have told you recently, with straight faces, the best way to get consumers to buy things is to avoid selling to them. Or 'only content that is worthless possesses value.' Or how about 'the more consumers get for free, the more money you'll make?'" says Baskin, who's quick to point out how many social media consultants *violate their own rules.*

"They usually provide a service, valued by demand, for which you have to pay," says Baskin, who wonders why these consultants don't take some of their own medicine: forsake payment in tangible currencies. Instead, he says they should agree to share in the "happy futurity of social karma that your business is supposed to value more."

"If your return can't be measured in dollars, why should theirs?" asks Baskin. "Let everybody get paid in acronyms of new media speak," jokes Baskin, who admits, "Obviously, this won't work for them because they *are*, in fact, subject to the laws of classical physics when providing their service."

Baskin (a bit of a modern day Galileo) has been relentlessly beating the behavior drum for a good few years. Having worked in marketing communications for large brands like Nissan and Apple, he's witnessed advertising's shortcomings and found comedy in its errors. He believes a fundamental shift in how marketing is executed is underway. The central tenets of mass media practices are under scrutiny. There's a power struggle, and social media marketing is caught in the middle.

Says Bob Hoffman, better known as the Ad Contrarian, "According to most new-age marketing gurus, there's apparently a whole new species of human being. This species has some interesting traits. First, other than the Internet, they don't trust media. They are immune to marketing. They dislike advertising, and they want to have conversations with brands. This, of course, is nonsense."

"But it's remarkable how widespread these beliefs have become," says Hoffman, who goes on to explain that research tells us that the Internet is the *least* trusted of major media sources and that *no one* is immune to marketing. Hoffman says to "just look in their refrigerator" for proof.

Hoffman points out that *nobody* has ever liked advertising, and they never will. And "as far as conversations go, most people are smart enough not to bother having conversations with their husbands—why the hell would they want to have conversations with brands?"

Rebooting Marketing

Over three decades ago, advertising legend David Ogilvy himself predicted this moment in time when he addressed direct-response marketers in India (www.oth.me/dogilvy). Ogilvy said, "There are two worlds—your world of direct response advertising and that other world. The world of general advertising. These two worlds are on a collision course."

In fact, Ogilvy passionately proclaimed, "You direct response people know what kind of advertising works and what doesn't work. You know it to a dollar. The general advertising people don't know."

Ogilvy was a guy who recommended that nobody be allowed to create general advertising without having studied and practiced direct response. He took shots at mass communications advertisers and agencies that, he said, "know almost nothing for sure because they cannot measure the results of their advertising." He was even wise enough to predict the demise of creativity as the basis of value in the advertising industry.

"You direct response people know what kind of advertising works and what doesn't work. You know it to a dollar. The general advertising people don't know."

"They worship at the altar of creativity, which really means originality, the most dangerous word in the lexicon of advertising," said Ogilvy, who also predicted what Daniel Morel of Wunderman and John Gerzema of Young and Rubicam are confirming. That is, practitioners of general advertising, as he called it, would start learning from direct marketers.

"The chasm between direct response advertising and general advertising is wide," said Ogilvy, who saw "no reason why direct response divisions of agencies should be separate from the main agencies."

And in a moment that must give Bob Hoffman and Jonathan Salem Baskin chills, Oglivy told direct response marketers, "You have it in your power to rescue the advertising business from its manifold lunacies."

In concluding his talk, an aging Oglivy said, "For forty years, I've been a voice crying in the wilderness, trying to get my fellow advertising practitioners to take direct response seriously. Today, my first love is coming into its own. You face a golden future."

This great mind foresaw electronic media coming of age. In his mind's eye, Ogilvy could see what's happening today, decades before it occurred. Given what he observed during his pioneering career, he was able to predict the merging of direct response with traditional brand advertising—the rise of what's being called "marketing science." But what he likely didn't see very clearly was how *long* it would take for his vision to materialize. Neither did he likely foresee the struggle we're undergoing, the turmoil involved in overcoming outdated habits and conditioning. But he did see the rise of marketing science based on what he was, at the time, able to plainly ***observe***.

Mixing in Direct Response

The exciting observations made possible by social media require a new approach. Indeed, one that relies less on mass media advertising ideas, yet without excluding it. We need a durable strategy that mixes in the direct response element. And as we've learned, some businesses have one. Yet many marketers are still "going the Ptolemy way"—applying old, mass media advertising practices in a new reality. And that's why so many of us are frustrated with the results we're getting.

For instance, Jonathan Salem Baskin says many misguided marketers are working on something "new" (that actually isn't) called engagement. They've become obsessed with defining it in terms of *time spent, content shared*, or whatever. As a result, Baskin says many are overlooking what *really* works, what's *always* worked—the traditional practices that "got to a sales result pretty quickly," in his words.

Okay, what really works? According to Baskin, it's this simple: Tell the truth, and tell it with relevance, immediacy, and meaning.

"That's why ads that interrupted with sales messages worked so effectively for so long," says Baskin. "Making the content worth consumers' time meant brands could risk asking for the sale."

> *Better observation urges us to change what we expect from social media marketing: its output. That means readjusting the model itself, making Web marketing more operationally observant and process-driven.*

Hmmm. Isn't that why, for instance, infomercials work?

I think of it this way: The ideas or rules governing mass advertising create a reluctance, a resistance to comprehend the "next step" social media marketing bestows upon us. Some who work in mass media advertising cannot easily understand or *appreciate* it simply based on their own routines and habits. On the other hand, some folks *do* appreciate it. They *fear* it. Both reactions are to be expected. Again, we're only human. But mixing in a bit of innovation and direct response marketing is a proven way to sell off the hook.

As we've discussed throughout this book, there is a clear answer. Better observation urges us to change what we expect from social media marketing: its output. And that means readjusting the model itself, making Web marketing more operationally observant and process-driven.

When Rok Hrastnik of Studio Moderna lectures, he uses a great image to illustrate the common sense urgency of this point. He flashes up an actual screenshot on a projection screen. It is an image of his e-mail inbox, and it shows a barrage of e-mail sent to him from Lands' End, a catalog company he ordered from. The times and dates of the e-mail messages sent by Lands' End can be plainly seen, and they're virtually nonstop. They're seen in his inbox, arriving daily and sometimes as often as twice daily. The barrage was so offensive to him (as a customer) that he uses it to make a dramatic point.

From	Subject	Received
Lands' End	Last Day for Free Shipping! + Save on swimwear	7.4.2009 13:07
Lands' End	Today only: 20% off 1000s of spring essentials	8.4.2009 6:11
Lands' End	Free Shipping on everything, limited time + 25% off all ...	9.4.2009 13:17
Lands' End	Free Shipping, no minimum + 25% off all swimwear thr...	10.4.2009 6:22
Lands' End	FREE SHIPPING, NO MINIMUM + 25% off swimsuits for...	11.4.2009 6:14
Lands' End	Free Shipping on everything + 25% off all swimwear - l...	12.4.2009 6:15
Lands' End	20% off sitewide one day only + $10 Tees, $15 Polos. ...	13.4.2009 12:47
Lands' End	Free Shipping, $10 Tees, $15 Polos - one more day!	14.4.2009 6:14
Lands' End	Last day: Free Shipping + $10 Tees, $15 Polos	15.4.2009 6:10
Lands' End	20% savings for 3 more days - shop now and save	17.4.2009 6:10
Lands' End	30% off site-wide for Friends & Family!	18.4.2009 1:16
Lands' End	30% off site-wide for Friends & Family. Only 3 days left!	18.4.2009 6:10
Lands' End	ENDS TODAY! 30% off site-wide for Friends & Family	20.4.2009 6:16
Lands' End	FREE SHIPPING on everything + 30% off all swim. 3 d...	21.4.2009 12:29
Lands' End	Free Shipping on everything, 25% off shoes & sandals ...	22.4.2009 6:18
Lands' End	Free Shipping + up to 40% off. Spring for it - only 3 da...	25.4.2009 11:26
Lands' End	Free Shipping, 25% off swim, even more on spring fav...	26.4.2009 6:21
Lands' End	Free Shipping + up to 40% off. Spring for it - only 2 da...	27.4.2009 0:47
Lands' End	Last Day: Free Shipping, up to 40% off favorites.	27.4.2009 6:23
Lands' End	Ends today! 30-50% off swimwear + Free Shipping	29.4.2009 6:17
Lands' End	Extended 1 day: 30-50% off swimwear + Free Shippin...	30.4.2009 6:16
Lands' End	FREE SHIPPING + $10 off select Fine Gauge cotton sw...	1.5.2009 13:24

Successful Web marketing is about *interaction*. And if that's true, this means that relying on frequency and repetition of outbound messages as a way to sell is limited. Said plainly, broadcasting to keep "in the face" or "top of mind" with customers isn't interacting with them. It's talking at them. In this case, Lands' End was messaging Hrastnik about a free shipping offer over and over and over within a week's time. Of course, Lands' End is a longstanding, sophisticated database marketer who would never send eleven or more pieces of direct mail to its customers' home per week. But in Hrastnik's case the cataloger was e-mailing at this offensive rate. Why?

Aside from e-mail being darn near free to deliver, this was happening because the professional in charge of e-mail was not thinking—or acting—as a translator. This person was a *broadcaster*, an advertiser. The man or woman whose decision it was to send these e-mails (so frequently) is tied to a mass media *values system* that believes (and invests) more in "reach-and-frequency"—to the exclusion of direct response marketing and behavioral observation.

You'll recall in our story about Hrastnik and Dormeo (chapter 4) that everything changed when his company stopped broadcasting and started interacting. The bedding brand started out broadcasting sleep-related e-mail newsletters to prospects, hoping for sales to materialize. It's a familiar, comfortable, and popular routine supported by years of habit. It's an accepted practice rooted in an outdated idea: "send more e-mail out, get more sales back in."

But it just doesn't work *well enough* anymore. Using a sweepstakes and highly valued, e-mail-delivered knowledge, Dormeo coaxed customers into *giving themselves a meaningful reason to interact* with the brand—a reason that had nearly nothing to do with the company's bedding products but a meaningful reason to customers nonetheless. Hrastnik's experience (and others I'm constantly featuring on www.offthehookblog.com) proves that people unfamiliar with a brand are willing to stomach occasional promotions from a seller, and if you don't get sloppy, they'll even *buy* your product or service! They'll transact if you avoid making too many annoying calls to action.

Just the same, some software companies are encouraging as many trial installations as possible. It's a numbers game. The more outbound messages they generate, the more trials might happen. And the more trials that happen increases chances of earning paying customers. That's absolutely true, and companies like HubSpot use free trials, too, but the real action lies in *expanding* the numbers game to include a *qualitative* aspect.

Does a company benefit from having as many of those interactive relationships as possible? Certainly! And HubSpot has over 11,000 in its rapidly-growing community. The point is this: Mixing in a problem-solving approach that grows sales is a more practical, effective way to get the job done. Observing customers and delicately making direct calls to action becomes a snap in an environment focused on teaching customers. In this light, the number of free downloads still matters. But it's the pairing of free trials with an observation, behavior-driven system that really kicks it into gear. Observing and translating customer behavior produces *more and better* leads. (and up-selling opportunities)

Is one strategy better than the other? Maybe. HubSpot tends to enjoy poking fun at mass media advertising. But no matter what your opinion is on the matter, winning businesses are *mixing in* direct approaches because it makes life easier. In most cases, this isn't about replacing mass media investments; rather, it's about *supplementing* them in ways that sell off the hook.

Consider Ikea's approach to its new store opening as compared to the way Burger King executed its Whopper Sacrifice campaign in earlier chapters. Take note of the expectation and outcome Burger King designed for. It created value in customers' lives in two ways—giving them a freebie and improving their Facebook experience. And for the restaurant, it drove customers into stores in a behaviorally and financially observable way. Ikea's "big idea" was to spread images of its store's products far and wide. Ikea's stated goal and outcome was limited to mass media constructs—"lots of views." It failed to build a useful marketing asset for itself—something the store could use over time to foster sales.

While most of us are broadcasting on the social Web, smart businesses are capturing sales with it. Large and small companies are mixing in traditional direct response concepts. They're observing and responding to customers' needs in appropriate, respectful, personalized ways, and in ways that don't rely exclusively on traditional advertising frameworks.

Breaking Free of Advertising's Confines

In 1990, Heather Gorringe started Wiggly Wigglers (www.wiggly wigglers.com) on her Herefordshire, UK, farm. There are "three times more cows than humans" in Blakemere, jokes Gorringe, who says the village is home to sixty-three people. But on a serious note, in 2006, Wiggly Wigglers cut spending on traditional advertising. Like so many small business owners were, Gorringe was forced to, and that's when she decided to focus on solving customers problems with digital publishing. As a result, her seventeen-employee company is managing to thrive despite the worst economic challenges in generations.

In the early days, Gorringe and her partners invested in traditional advertising to get the word out. Wiggly Wigglers started up as a natural gardening mail-order company, and since the beginning they've been selling products that gardeners may not (yet) know that they want.

"Like worm composting kits to take kitchen waste and turn it into compost," says Gorringe, who views the company as being different than a conventional garden center. Lately, they've expanded into flowers, plants, and eco-friendly homeware. But they've always been focused on niche products—solutions to problems that often take time to materialize in customers' lives.

Today, Wiggly Wigglers is an international, social media–driven e-commerce business—complete with a growing customer database of 70,000 e-mail newsletter subscribers. About 7 percent of new customers are coming from Facebook and Twitter. The company's podcast has thousands of listeners from all around the world and scores of 5-star reviews on iTunes.

The Wiggly team produces frequent, lively, information-rich programs covering the environment, wildlife, gardening, farming, and biodiversity. Recently, the business began to publish short, tips-based video programs, too. Prospective and current customers are gobbling up the free, high-quality, high-energy advice.

The company's pioneering work in social marketing is even winning small business grants from the likes of Dell Corporation. That's helping fuel growth as the company makes needed investments in warehouse and back office infrastructure. Wiggly Wigglers is expanding, but life wasn't always sunshine and flowers.

Testing the Waters

In order to turn a profit, mail-order businesses historically buy lists of potential customers and mail them. It can get expensive, and Wiggly Wigglers was no different. In early days, the business invested heavily in both direct mail and advertising. Gorringe and her partners were a start-up trying to build a small, regionally focused business.

By the mid-nineties, the company had its e-commerce Web site up and running alongside of a print catalog. By 2005, the company began experimenting with podcasts. Why? The answer is multifaceted, but Gorringe had a hunch.

"No one is going to wake up in the morning and say, 'Ah-ha! I really need to compost my kitchen waste using worms,'" smiles Gorringe, who believes much of what she sells requires an educational approach to gardening. She's quick to note that small farmers and gardeners have grown to expect something for nothing, namely useful tips and tricks from people they can trust. Customers expect to buy from sellers who are educated about gardening and genuinely likable. They also expect sellers to be available, "always on" and in formats customers find useful—like blogs they can read, podcasts they can listen to on the run (www.wigglywigglers.co.uk/podcasts), and short video clips they can view (www.wigglywigglers.co.uk/cinema).

As chance had it, the Wiggly team started podcasting because the company couldn't get any good, local radio coverage. Although Gorringe's quick wit and expertise made her a popular interviewee for local radio shows, her clips were often cut short—focused on news, not helpful gardening tips.

Thanks to this relatively trivial problem and simple tools like iTunes, Gorringe discovered podcasting. Wiggly Wigglers made a £2500 investment in podcasting over 10 weeks. The team promoted it with some success locally and within iTunes. In essence, Gorringe tested the waters.

When Life Gives You Worms, Make Lively Advice

Good thing she did. The massive, global economic slowdown beginning around 2008 forced Wiggly Wigglers to slow down even more. Like so many businesses across the globe, this one was forced to react to sudden market change. Gorringe pulled the reigns in and tightened everything up. She reduced the size of her catalog, which had tripled in size the year before.

Wiggly Wigglers' products were never an obvious "must have." The company was always ahead of the curve with eco-friendly and green products. But suddenly customers began purchasing based on needs, not wants. The problem was compounded by Wiggly Wiggler's competitors' answer to reduced demand: deep discounting.

Of course, getting known remained critical, and that's when the team decided to focus *even more* on solving customers' problems. Gorringe decided to stick with social media. Why? Because there was too much at stake. As a result, Wiggly Wigglers is becoming more known "organically." Indeed, internationally. Gorringe's hunch was right—customers crave innovative, new solutions to age-old problems. She was able to observe some exciting behavior. Wiggly Wigglers's helpful eco-conscious tips, gardening advice, and products were becoming known far and wide.

"We're obsessed with social media, and there's only one reason why: it's because it's incredibly inexpensive for us to get out there and get word-of-mouth, global conversation going about our company and our products and the changes we're able to make in people's gardens," says Gorringe, whose passion for gardening is palpable within a few seconds of hearing her speak, perhaps unlike her competitors.

You see, after pulling back on advertising, Wiggly Wigglers immediately invested a third of the recovered savings in *nurturing* niche markets with online publishing. Gorringe admits it was risky. But like Studio Moderna's Hrastnik, she continually measures, observes, and improves her returns, and she's experiencing enough success to justify continued investment.

Wiggly Wigglers made a practical wager. This small, farm-based business bet that educating a niche market in ways that solved problems would spread across the Web, and it did.

Observing and Nurturing Niches

Today, Wiggly Wigglers is podcasting, vlogging (video blogging), microblogging (Twitter and Facebook), and text blogging—publishing in multiple formats through multiple channels—and they're still doing it out of necessity. It just makes sense.

For instance, Wiggly Wigglers needs *time* to convince prospects that it *is* worth buying certain products. How do they know this? It's what they observe in customers' behavior. As an example, consider Wiggly's British-origin bouquets. This is one of their niche products. Of course, flowers can be purchased easily online though hundreds (if not thousands) of sources. But it takes time to explain subtle differences between British bouquets and those from other regions.

Time is also needed when courting an expanding list of customer types on the idea of worm farming, another niche. Urban and rural gardeners, bird-watching enthusiasts, and nature-loving, eco-conscious parents of children—they're all budding customer groups that need nurturing. And that's precisely what the company is accessing when it uses online publishing tools like podcasts and blogs. Yet there's something more practical that factors into this company's decision making. Wiggly Wigglers is observing powerful behavior of those consuming its content.

"All of our blogs, audio, and video programs last for years," says Gorringe. "The initial investment is low, and we love, love, love doing them. They've given us the confidence needed to slash our conventional advertising budget."

"Once a business is producing content, it costs no more to offer it to more people. Also, the tables are turned a bit. When customers would rather not receive content (be part of the Facebook group, a Twitter follower, or a podcast listener), then they opt out. This makes the customers that stay really valuable. And so I'm happy to invest in them for as long as it takes, as it costs no more," says Gorringe.

The Wiggly Wigglers catalog remains in print. It's just smaller, more focused on emerging gardening niches, and it's now aided by the merchandising prowess of the company's customer base. Through use of a wiki and various other feedback devices, customers help Gorringe's team keep **constantly** synchronized with products that matter most. Wiggly Wigglers is forever relevant, in context with its niche customer base, all because of its supercharged ability to **observe** what customers are doing, saying, and contributing.

Measure to Observe and Optimize Sales

Today, Wiggly Wigglers is in growth mode. Gorringe's initial hunch was right. Giving customers innovative, new solutions to age-old problems can grow a business. Social media, solution selling, and direct response marketing are a perfect fit. Yes, she attributes a lot of Wiggly Wigglers' success to a quirky, fun-loving, honestly unique business culture. But Gorringe is also a marketing scientist who's discovered a practical way to observe, measure, and improve social media's output. She is making social media marketing more process-driven, operational, and productive.

"I think in any business, data management is really important," says Gorringe. "I don't like this idea of segmenting everyone into a perfect label. But I *do* like the practical idea of recording what people are interested in and delivering it to them and being able to make sure they don't end up with junk mail and spam."

In an interview with UK blogger Juliet Fay (www.onlinesalesmessages .com), Gorringe discusses how she delivers two newsletters per month (she since increased to twice weekly) to subscribers. Just as she does in Facebook, she makes bold but respectful calls to action. She adds promotions to information-rich e-mails that generate responses. Within a minute's time, Gorringe can be heard on the interview firing up her e-mail analytics software, finding her most successful e-mail campaign's statistics. She's fearless that way! Wiggly Wiggler's Summer Sale newsletter generated a 20 percent open rate and 6 percent click-through rate. She then logs in to Google Analytics to reveal her e-commerce site's 2,761 visits and $70,541.49 in sales for the day.

Gorringe's success proves that one doesn't need be a technical genius to make social media pay business dividends. You just need a focused *purpose* for the tools you're using, and you need to be observing, learning from and acting on customer behavior. After all, Web marketing as a whole gives us "observational superiority," and that fact urges us to change what we expect from social media marketing—its output. It's time to expect sales.

I Can See Clearly Now

Think of the last few years like watching a sporting event or music concert from the upper balcony. Well, now is your chance to move to a box seat on the main floor. By applying what you've learned in this book, you'll start to feel more effective, as if you are part of the action—like you *are* the action, and that's because you *will* be more effective.

"It's not about companies being at the center or not, changing the rules or any of the other glib blah-blah that passes for conclusions," says global brand strategist Jonathan Salem Baskin, who reminds us that Galileo's observations made reality *clearer*, not bigger.

"Marketers themselves are the advocates for truly new understanding. They're the ones putting interactive, behavior-based theories to test—in the same universe in which laws of gravity and the speed of light still apply," says Baskin.

I agree. And I hope you do, too, because the observations being made by the people we've met together aren't much different from Galileo's in terms of their power. Consider how observing customers helps entrepreneur Ryan Safady drive more sales and how it's making his products more relevant to practical (J and O Fabrics) and emotional (Imagine Lifestyles) customers. Consider how observing and *prompting* behavior is creating more outcomes, more reliably and more often for his businesses. Entrepreneurs like Safady are spurring the rest of us to update our *expectation* of a new interactive marketing model.

But where to start? I've given you specific next steps to consider, but as you approach them, it's critical to remember that the answers we seek in life are almost always found by asking different, better questions.

I'm continually asked how many blog posts are needed to make the exercise effective; how often must updates be posted to a Facebook fan page to see a return and how much Twitter engagement is needed to realize positive effect. Nobel questions, all, but they intersect with measurement of influence as *popularity or attention*, and that's precisely the problem. These are the wrong questions.

Yes, we ask them because they're familiar and comfortable. But these are questions that our old, outdated mass communications *habits* encourage us to ask. As we've seen throughout this book, mastering social selling demands we ask different, *better* questions.

You're now ready to put social media marketing to better use. It's time to focus more on your strengths and start expecting more of social media marketing because your observations are, today, already providing a more usable reality. I hope this book makes you feel readier and abler to begin designing processes around customers' behavior like never before—ways to help them navigate toward your products and services.